Praise for *Leader in Me*

What Thought Leaders Are Saying

"*Leader in Me* is one of the most inspired efforts taking hold today in our schools. Sean Covey beautifully tells the story and elegantly explains the process's principles and promise. If you care about education, you need to read this book."
—Daniel H. Pink, #1 *New York Times* bestselling author of *Drive*, *To Sell Is Human*, and *The Power of Regret*

"Far more often than not, young people live up to high expectations—when those expectations have personal meaning. In a time when the endgame in schools can be little more than a standardized test score, *Leader in Me* helps young learners see their potential to develop a vision for who they can become, take charge of their lives, work with peers to solve problems, and make positive decisions about their well-being. The process reminds them that learning can and should be magical, and that pursuit of quality extends both learning and the learner. The process's habits of success, which, on some level, are affective and environmental aspects of learning success, integrate seamlessly into academic content as well, endowing that content with extended purpose and meaning—for students and teachers alike."
—Dr. Carol Ann Tomlinson, William Clay Parrish Jr. Professor Emerita, University of Virginia, School of Education & Human Development, and author of *So Each May Soar: The Principles and Practices of Learner-Centered Classrooms*

"Educators are doing their very best to meet the challenges that accompany our schools today. They are passionate about education and are deeply committed to their students' success. But they cannot do it alone. The *Leader in Me* process offers schools and educators the opportunity to build a strong culture of student empowerment and self-discipline, so that students are taking responsibility for their own education and success. It is so inspiring to see the success in numerous schools throughout the world that have employed the process and whose students are becoming twenty-first-century leaders in their own right."
—Dr. Daniel Domenech, former Executive Director, American Association of School Administrators, The School Superintendents Association

"*The Leader in Me* is a wonderful book—relevant, thoughtful, and enormously useful. The core ideas are presented through an engaging array of stories, narratives, examples, and photographs of real schools. This book should be on the shelf of every school that wants to be successful, caring, and serving every child in their community."
—Dr. Kent D. Peterson, Professor Emeritus, University of Wisconsin–Madison, and coauthor of *Shaping School Culture: Pitfalls, Paradoxes, and Promises*

"External efforts to perk up schools have failed. They miss the secret of success. A cohesive culture, developed within a local school, unites teachers, students, parents, and the community in a common quest of making learning meaningful and joyful. *The Leader in Me* demonstrates vividly through stories and testimony how schools can reclaim soul and spirit."
—Terrence Deal, coauthor of *Shaping School Culture: Pitfalls, Paradoxes, and Promises* and *How Great Leaders Think*

"Working with thousands of students over the years opened my eyes to the 'untaught lessons' of contemporary education: do what you're told; look good on paper; and seek external validation. I spent years watching brilliant young people feel they were anything but brilliant because their particular approach to adding value to the world couldn't be adequately measured or rewarded through essays and written tests. *Leader in Me* creates a different culture in schools. It asks students and staff to assess and do what they think is right, to empower themselves and others, and to recognize and foster the existing capacities for greatness within themselves. Perhaps most important, it creates rewards that are accessible to each and every student. Ultimately, the greatest endorsement for *Leader in Me* is to meet the students who have been impacted by its approach. They are, quite simply, different. Nowhere else in the world have I met students with the confidence and passion of those I've met from *Leader in Me* schools. I once asked a young man from a *Leader in Me* school, 'What do you hope the future will bring?' With a smile, he confidently replied, 'Big things.' Consider making the *Leader in Me* a part of your school's culture. You, too, can expect big things."
—Drew Dudley, founder and chief catalyst of Day One Leadership, Inc., and *Wall Street Journal* bestselling author of *This Is Day One: A Practical Guide to Leadership That Matters*

"I have personally visited A.B. Combs Elementary and was blown away by the mature student body that greeted and interviewed me. This school is a phenomenal example of how an institution can take *Leader in Me*, build upon the *7 Habits*, and prepare students for their undefined futures. This book proves that there truly is greatness in every student and in every staff member, and that through this process, greatness can be realized."

—Jeff Jones, Executive Chairman of Solution Tree; cofounder of Marzano Resources

"I believe the children of today will become our leaders tomorrow. I believe we need to prepare our children to be the kind of leaders who will create a brighter and better future. I believe in *Leader in Me*. It's the book, process, and pathway to develop leaders that will positively transform our schools, communities, and future."

—Jon Gordon, bestselling author of *The Energy Bus* and *The Energy Bus for Kids*

"As schools go, so goes our future. Educated, self-disciplined, civil adults are first educated, self-disciplined, and civil students. Like the sand that polishes the stone, school experiences bring forth the brilliance hidden within each child. *Leader in Me* is based on a mindset of a better world and a comprehensive set of proven principles to get us there. I strongly recommend this framework to all educational leaders striving to advance the 'learning for all' mission."

—the late Lawrence W. Lezotte, effective schools consultant

"*The Leader in Me* tells how the process is transforming schools, one school at a time, and is changing the lives of students around the world. Every child has the individual potential and worth to succeed in life and to accomplish any goal they set. If they have teachers who inspire them and believe in them, they will come to see in themselves that they are leaders, not just today, but for the rest of their lives. Truly, a remarkable book and process."

—Ron Clark, founder and teacher at the Ron Clark Academy; author of *Be 1% Better: Surprisingly Simple Ways to Transform Your School*, *Move Your Bus*, and *The Excellent 11: An Award-Winning Teacher's Guide to Motivate, Inspire, and Educate Kids*

"*Leader in Me* is at the core of my formula for changing the culture of the toughest schools in America! One small part of Stephen Covey's huge legacy will be his inspirational message on leadership to children, teachers, and administrators around the world. Sean Covey has continued to carry the torch of leadership for young people in a powerful way! You want true school reform—read *The Leader in Me*!"

—Salome Thomas-EL, EdD, award-winning principal and author of *Meet Their Needs and They'll Succeed*

"*Leader in Me*, the culmination of something exciting in our schools, began at a school in North Carolina where they dreamed of what was possible for students. Muriel Summers and Sean Covey together create a new nexus we haven't seen in schools. They challenge us to reflect on our core values and nurture those of the young people we serve. As educators, and especially educators in magnet schools, we are acutely aware of the limitless possibilities in every student. *Leader in Me* shows a path to engage and support students in ways that will lead to extraordinary opportunities. All students need to understand how to not only harness their potential but simultaneously serve in capacities that will force them to know who they are and what they stand for. Our country will depend on these leaders, and educators can devote themselves to inspiring and training the leaders we need for tomorrow. *Leader in Me* had applications that went far beyond the classroom and, as a parent, gave me incredible insight and ways to guide the development of my own children."

—Scott Thomas, former Executive Director, Magnet Schools of America

What Parents and Community Leaders Are Saying

"As a parent of two boys who have attended several schools, I can say without hesitation that Legacy Point Elementary and its *Leader in Me* approach have been truly transformational for my children. The *7 Habits* have not only been integrated into their daily routines but have also shaped their character, mindset, confidence, and sense of responsibility in ways no other school has. The reflective practices, leadership opportunities, and emphasis on life skills have empowered both of my sons to see themselves as capable, confident leaders. I believe the foundations they are building will have a positive, lasting impact on both of them. Finding Legacy Point felt like finding a home—it laid the foundation for their elementary years in the most meaningful, positive way. I am deeply grateful for the impact this process has had on their growth and development."

—Melissa Fitzgibbon, parent, Legacy Point Elementary, Colorado

"As a parent of two daughters (ten and six) I strive for them to grow not only academically but in character too. I am so gratefully surprised to have noticed such growth in both of them from learning and implementing the *Leader in Me* habits. This year, my eldest daughter was faced with a situation where the right thing to do was not the easiest. She came to me to talk it through, and it was so rewarding to hear how what she had learned was the driving force behind her discomfort and determination to make the matter right. The next day, she returned home happy and confident, realizing that being 'proactive' in standing up against meanness felt much more rewarding than being silent. My six-year-old stood up in front of her elementary school assembly and proudly shared what she had learned and even asked the audience questions! Both girls have flourished and are still shy but building confidence in the area of leadership. I could not be prouder. Thank you, *Leader in Me*!"

—Giovanna Smith, parent, Somerset Academy Sky Pointe, Nevada

"*Leader in Me* has provided a gold standard for our children to understand what it takes to be a leader; it has also laid a firm foundation, creating a path for success for their futures. This process has changed the lives of so many children, and beyond that, has had a significant impact on entire family units in our community. Children have been empowered and are leading by example, all of which might not have been possible without the influence and culture of *Leader in Me*."

—Dr. Breca Tracy, parent, Dripping Springs ISD, Texas

"The leadership process is exactly what my son needed to get back on track. He started developing a proactive attitude toward his schoolwork. Assignments were completed and turned in on time. Putting First Things First, he completed his math work almost always at school. Each week, we could see his confidence growing, and he went from being fearful and unsure of himself to being confident and empowered. Socially and athletically, he is very competitive but has developed a win-win approach and is able to synergize through class problems and group projects. When given the opportunity to take responsibility for his own actions, he did just that. We are forever grateful."

—Lori Helmy, parent, Mukilteo Elementary, Washington

"When my ninth grader asks to play a video game before his homework is done, I enjoy hearing my kindergartner pipe up and say, 'Put first things first, do your homework!'"

—Ericka Porrazza, parent, Lehua Elementary School, Hawaii

"As a parent in Pakistan, I have long hoped for an education system that nurtures not only academic success but also personal responsibility and emotional intelligence. When our children's school adopted *Leader in Me*, I witnessed a remarkable transformation in my children and the learning environment in school. This process cultivates leadership from an early age, impacting the whole family. As a family, we now strive to find win-win solutions in challenging situations. In a country where leadership development is often overlooked, this initiative is essential. *Leader in Me* fills a critical gap in our education system, developing future leaders and helping build a brighter future together."

—Rushdah Fatima, parent, Pakistan

"My joy in seeing my son as a confident, influential leader—ambitious, passionate about learning, and driven by his talents—is far greater than the joy I feel when I see an A next to his subjects on a report card. That's exactly what *Leader in Me* nurtures: years of continuous planting and growth with no pause."

Zainab Hashemi, parent, Britus International School, Egypt

"*Leader in Me* has made all the difference in my daughters' development. They use the Leadership Notebook to set and track their goals, which has greatly strengthened their organization and sense of responsibility. In our daily routine at home, we constantly talk about 'Putting First Things First,' prioritizing what truly matters. I am also pleasantly surprised at how naturally they have adopted the habit of resolving conflicts with a win-win mindset. Without a doubt, this process develops skills for a lifetime. I see it as essential in shaping children. It's the differentiator that helps them learn to relate to others and solve their problems independently, along with fostering a strong sense of responsibility. Surely, this will be a defining factor in their adult lives."

Daniela Pecoraro Moscardini de Aguiar, parent,
Colégio Educandário Anglo School, Brazil

"As a parent, *Leader in Me* has been a remarkable experience to witness through my son Yatharth Agrawal's journey at Zebar School for Children in Ahmedabad. I've seen him become more confident, responsible, and focused—not just in academics, but in how he approaches everyday challenges. The *7 Habits* have helped him think ahead, set personal goals, and collaborate better with others. It's incredibly fulfilling to see such values being developed at a young age. *Leader in Me* has truly brought a positive change in his mindset and behavior, and I'm grateful for the lasting impact it's making."

—Monika Agrawal, parent, Zebar School for Children, India

"The *7 Habits* have been a positive influence in my children's lives and in my own life. Once I was trying to tell my son, 'You're not listening, you're not

being proactive.' But then he said to me, 'Mom, you are not listening to me. You are being reactive.' And I had a huge paradigm shift, a moment of 'Oh my goodness, it is me.' So it is a two-way street. It has been really good for us, really good."
—Megan May, parent, Crestwood Elementary, Medicine Hat, Alberta, Canada

"Throughout my career as a businessman, I have had the privilege of working alongside and learning from remarkable leaders. When my community expressed a desire to implement *Leader in Me* in our public schools, I was initially skeptical about teaching leadership skills in an educational setting. However, during a business trip to North Carolina, I visited A.B. Combs Elementary School. After engaging with Principal Summers, teachers, and students, my skepticism quickly transformed into excitement. I realized that if *Leader in Me* could completely revitalize the school culture there, it could do wonders for the public schools in my hometown of Macon, Georgia.

"That trip was ten years ago. Today, I am proud to share that all our public schools actively practice the *7 Habits*. Over the past decade, I have witnessed a remarkable transformation in our schools. Students now arrive at school with a clear understanding of why they need to learn, recognizing that the leadership skills they cultivate will unlock incredible opportunities in their futures.

"Thanks to the implementation of *Leader in Me*, leadership is no longer just a concept; it is a driving force that is actively transforming my community. It is an honor for me to see our students grow into confident leaders, ready to make a positive impact in the world. This journey has not only enriched their lives but also strengthened the fabric of our community, giving me great hope for the next generation."
—Blake Sullivan, President and owner of Sullivan Forestry Consultants, Inc.

"Over sixty-two years of managing money, before I invest in any company, I want to understand the culture driving its employees. So, when I heard about *Leader in Me* and what it had done for Muriel Summers' school in Atlanta, I saw that it was a game changer and decided to introduce *Leader in Me* to schools in Allentown and Bethlehem. What good is all that learning if you don't have the knowledge of how to be successful? To be successful, the *Leader in Me* culture teaches how to take that learning and produce a happy, creative, and useful life."
—Al Douglass, Senior Vice President, The Douglass Group

"When I walked into A.B. Combs in 2007, I knew immediately that something was different. In my years of serving the education community, I have walked into countless schools on behalf of LEGO Education solutions. However, this was the first time I was greeted by a second-grade student who introduced herself, welcomed me to the school, inquired about my purpose for visiting, and offered to take me to see the principal, Ms. Muriel Summers. I was enthralled. As I came to know more of the school, the remarkable work of Muriel and her team, and, more important, the outcomes achieved by the students repeatedly and reliably, I learned about the unique implementation of Stephen Covey's *7 Habits*. I was well-versed in these habits, having added them to my leadership toolset, skillset, and mindset early on in my career. Seeing them implemented in such a school-wide setting encompassing the entire range of the child's experience, confirmed what I already knew. If the culture is right, the results will be right. If your goals are to prepare students for the twenty-first-century workforce, you know that deep content, twenty-first-century skills, hands-on learning, and a culture of respect and leadership are the keys to success. The *Leader in Me* process is a crown jewel in the transformation of school culture, freeing children to imagine, learn, and succeed."

—Stephan Turnipseed, former President and Executive
Director, Strategic Partnerships, LEGO Education US

What Educators Are Saying

"At Pryor Public Schools, students learn the *Leader in Me* habits in elementary school, apply them in more depth during middle school, and live them out at the high school level. Our sustained, district-wide implementation of the process contributes to the success of our students across the district and helps produce graduates who are ready to succeed in post-secondary education, the military, or the workforce."

—Dr. Lisa Muller, Superintendent, Pryor Public Schools, Oklahoma

"As a teacher first and now an assistant superintendent in a growing district of nearly 19,000 students, I am grateful for the opportunity to witness the transformative impact of *Leader in Me* over the past fifteen years. Students immersed in the *Leader in Me* culture consistently demonstrate strong leadership skills, including effective communication, collaboration, innovation, and confidence.

I have personally seen students lead new initiatives, one of which evolved into a company serving homeless veterans and others in need. Students have taken action to support those affected by natural disasters across the community and nation, and individuals facing life's unexpected tragedies. I have watched achievements grow in environments where students are confident and exhibit leadership skills.

In my role as assistant superintendent, it has been inspiring to watch preschoolers grow into graduates who are prepared to lead the world with the confidence and leadership abilities essential for navigating the future."

Dr. Sarah Johnson, Assistant Superintendent,
Warren County Public Schools, Kentucky

"*Leader in Me* has been nothing short of transformational for our school community. What began as a framework for instilling leadership habits has evolved into a shared mindset—a lens through which we view the world, approach challenges, and pursue goals with purpose and integrity. It has reshaped the culture of our school, empowering both students and staff to lead with intention, take ownership of their growth, and build meaningful relationships rooted in trust and mutual respect."

—Donna Walker Thompson, Principal, Northeast High School, Georgia

"*Leader in Me* is sometimes characterized as being for elementary schools. We have found that its principles and systems can have a significant positive influence at the high school level also. At its core, *Leader in Me* is about leadership, character, and building strong relationships. Over the past decade of living the *7 Habits* in our school, *Leader in Me* has shown it has the ability to better equip our students for the rigors of high school and the challenges and opportunities they will face after graduation."

—Fielding Elseman, Principal, Pryor High School, Oklahoma

"*Leader in Me* is a way of life that extends far beyond the classroom walls. As a principal who experienced it firsthand, I saw the powerful impact it had on our students and families. The leadership skills it nurtured brought out the best in our community and united us through a shared sense of purpose. I've also witnessed its influence at home, as my own child has begun applying these principles in everyday life. Seeing its transformative power in so many areas has been the most rewarding experience of my career."

—Brett Shelby, Principal, Dr. Bryan C. Jack Elementary, Texas

"*Leader in Me* is not a program, but a shift in culture in the school. It is a road map to build, grow, and cultivate an exciting, student-led school where kids not only are in charge of their own education, but their lives!"

—Cris Edwards, Principal, Richland County Elementary School, Illinois

"*Leader in Me* is a transformational experience like none other I have been part of in my thirty-three-year career. I believe every child, educator, parent, and community member continues to grow toward self-actualization as much as they are nurtured by systems that support this process. *Leader in Me* enables this to happen, one person at a time, to impact the entire community. The heart of this framework is love and celebration. When we love and celebrate who we are, who we work alongside, and what we achieve together, anything is possible."
—Denise Lessard, Principal, Battery Creek High School, South Carolina

"*Leader in Me* has helped our school discover a united purpose and shared goals. We have a shared vocabulary of growth from our youngest students to our most tenured staff that positively impacts behavioral and academic outcomes."
—Ben Frasier, Principal, Plano Elementary, Kentucky

"*Leader in Me* has truly transformed our school! Our first through third grade leaders, many of whom come from challenging home situations, excel in their use of the *7 Habits* and the leadership tools that are embedded in this process. *Leader in Me* empowers our children to lead themselves and others as they tap into their individual gifts. Through this process, educators celebrate the leadership ability in *all* children, much of which was not typically recognized in schools. I cannot envision school without this life-changing process that serves as the foundation of our daily work!"
—Dr. Kim Cummins, Principal, Martin Petitjean Elementary, Louisiana

"*Leader in Me* has been a game-changer in our school community. I've watched students grow into confident, compassionate leaders who take ownership of their actions and believe in their potential. It's more than a program—it's a mindset that empowers every child to lead with purpose and heart. I truly believe this work is shaping a brighter future, one student at a time."
—Jessica Pellegrino, Assistant Principal, Greater
Latrobe Senior High School, Pennsylvania

"As both a mother and a principal, I've seen *Leader in Me* make a powerful impact on children's confidence, responsibility, and leadership. The process transforms school culture by empowering students to take ownership of their learning and actions. It nurtures a sense of purpose, builds strong character, and inspires every child to lead."
—Juley Sexton, Principal, A.B. Combs Elementary, North Carolina

"*Leader in Me* fits well into our district's belief in educating the whole child. We want to graduate well-rounded students who are compassionate, competitive, critical thinkers, and lifelong learners. The *Leader in Me* is helping us to make it a reality."
—Pat Sanford, Leadership Development Specialist, North East Independent School District, San Antonio, Texas

"We have implemented *Leader in Me* from day one of opening the doors of our school. The formal training of our staff and incorporation of the *7 Habits* into subject lessons has worked in tandem to create a culture of trust, accountability, and leadership among our staff and student body. This led directly to our school's designation as the number one school in New York City Public Schools, as measured by the Department of Education's Progress Report."
—Rose Kerr, founding Principal, Staten Island School of Civic Leadership, New York

"In only two weeks we saw dramatic changes, from both staff and parent perspectives. After five months of implementing *Leader in Me* with students, we have seen an 85 percent decrease in behavior referrals."
—Deirdre Brady, Principal, Heritage Elementary, Michigan

"'*Leader in Me* is not about doing things differently but about seeing things differently.' Muriel Summers has nailed it down so well, and in my view, this is the core philosophy of *Leader in Me*. Habib Public School (Karachi, Pakistan) chose to introduce *Leader in Me* in 2022, and we are so enthusiastic about using the right paradigms and processes. A combination of *The 7 Habits of Highly Effective People* and *The 4 Disciplines of Execution* is the right mix for an excellent educational institution. Through the L.I.M. process, we are striving to strengthen our school's philosophy of 'Making Learning Fun.'"
—Minhas Tejani, Principal, Habib Public School and High School, Pakistan

"The experience of implementing *Leader in Me* reveals its profound impact on students, staff, and the entire school community. It empowers students to cultivate essential leadership skills by emphasizing personal responsibility, goal setting, and teamwork, all through the integration of *The 7 Habits of Highly Effective People* into the curriculum. Overall, the process fosters not only academic success but also the development of character and leadership qualities that prepare students for future challenges."
—Abeer Hammoud, educator, Najd National School, Egypt

"We work with children on the autism spectrum, ADHD, trauma, and various conditions, who have experienced so much failure and no longer feel valued. With *Leader in Me*, they learn and experience who they really are—that they are of value. By applying the *7 Habits*, they become increasingly aware of their own abilities and learn that they can choose how to act, even in difficult situations—they regulate their emotions and find more positive ways to act and feel. Through this process, we see them grow in confidence, finding their voice, and believing in themselves."

> —Seleke Steehouwer-Kaashoek, Coordinator Special Needs,
> Buitengewoon Onderwijs Foundation, The Netherlands

"As an educator, I see daily the positive impact of *Leader in Me* on our students' development. It promotes essential social-emotional skills for life, strengthening their ability to build healthy relationships at home, at school, and within the community. Our students understand their roles in society and recognize their responsibility for their choices and their consequences. They learn to plan their lives, set priorities, and respect differences, which significantly contributes to bullying prevention and the creation of a more welcoming environment. We are shaping conscious, ethical, and responsible leaders who will undoubtedly become adults capable of transforming society. This gives us hope and confidence in a better future."

> —Patrícia Pereira, educator, educational psychologist, and author of the
> book *Lições de Liderança Começam em Casa* (Leadership
> Lessons Start at Home), Colégio Anglo Morumbi School, Brazil

"*Leader in Me* cultivates a positive, student-centric school culture where each student is empowered as a leader, benefiting the entire school community. At Shanti Asiatic School, it is equipping students with crucial life and leadership skills—including responsibility, goal setting, collaboration, and self-confidence—while simultaneously enhancing academic performance and improving student behavior. For teachers, it has been providing a unified framework for teaching leadership skills, improving classroom management, and strengthening teacher-student relationships. In summary, it is transforming the school into a collaborative community founded on mutual respect, empowerment, and shared progress."

> —Abhay Ghosh, Director, Shanti Asiatic School, India

"I received *The Leader in Me* from a friend on my way to a winter holiday. Its message touched me so deeply that I couldn't go relax before I had read the entire book! It has truly enabled greatness in all aspects of my life, in my family, and in my schools."

—Lise K. Furuseth, founder, Hoppensprett Schools
and Day Care Centres, Norway

"With a risk-taker hat and a desire to innovate and bring positive change, we implemented *Leader in Me*. The process adds value to the school's 'end in mind' of strengthening children's character and provides them with the right environment for personal and academic growth. The emphasis on each child's worth strengthens them as unique individuals and reinforces their self-confidence and their desire to 'synergize' and to build a better world."

—the late Martha Rincón, former Director,
Buckingham School, Bogotá, Colombia

"When I observe children these days, sometimes I feel they lack certain skills, like interpersonal skills or teamwork skills. Their parents are busy, their families tend to be small, and they have tons of homework. As a result, they do not have the chance to interact with other children or to develop these skills through play. So as a teacher, I feel privileged to teach skills like 'think win-win' and 'synergy!' They help students to be more effective as students and better able to handle life's challenges."

—Mrs. Limmengkwang, teacher, Chua Chu Kang Primary, Singapore

The Leader in Me

First published in the United States by Simon & Schuster,
an imprint of Simon & Schuster, LLC, 2025

First published in Great Britain by Simon & Schuster UK Ltd, 2026

1 3 5 7 9 10 8 6 4 2

Simon & Schuster UK Ltd
1st Floor
222 Gray's Inn Road
London WC1X 8HB

www.simonandschuster.co.uk
www.simonandschuster.com.au
www.simonandschuster.co.in

Simon & Schuster Australia, Sydney
Simon & Schuster India, New Delhi

The authorised representative in the EEA is Simon & Schuster Netherlands BV,
Herculesplein 96, 3584 AA Utrecht, Netherlands. info@simonandschuster.nl

A CIP catalogue record for this book is available from the British Library

Trade Paperback ISBN: 978-1-3985-6540-1
eBook ISBN: 978-1-3985-6541-8

Printed and Bound in the UK using 100% Renewable
Electricity at CPI Group (UK) Ltd

The Leader in Me

3rd Edition

How Schools and Parents Around the World Are
Inspiring Greatness, One Student at a Time

Stephen R. Covey

Sean Covey

Muriel Summers

David K. Hatch

SIMON & SCHUSTER

London · New York · Amsterdam/Antwerp · Sydney/Melbourne · Toronto · New Delhi

*For teachers,
administrators, parents, and community leaders
who are searching for a fresh and inspiring
approach to education.
And especially
for students.*

What Is Inside

Dr. Covey lived by the motto "Live life in crescendo," always believing and living as if his greatest contribution was yet ahead, including *Leader in Me*.

In Tribute

Just prior to reaching the young age of eighty, Dr. Stephen R. Covey announced he had a new motto: Live life in crescendo! "I live each day," he said, "as if my best contribution is yet ahead."

At that point in his life, it was hard to imagine what Dr. Covey might do to surpass what he had already contributed to the world. His book *The 7 Habits of Highly Effective People* had reached over forty million readers.[1] Leaders from virtually every country were spreading his leadership principles across their organizations. Presidents of nations were reaching out to him and drawing on his wisdom. People's lives were being changed. What more of a legacy could he possibly leave?

What was on Dr. Covey's mind was the new book he had published in 2009, the first edition of *The Leader in Me*. He had visions of the *7 Habits* being taken to every student and every corner of the world. Thankfully, before an unfortunate bike accident took his life, Dr. Covey was able to see his vision starting to take root. That vision has now spread to more than eight thousand schools in over sixty countries. And so we pay tribute to Dr. Covey and his vision that continues to spread across the globe.

Dr. Covey would be the first to pass the tribute to a global community of passionate teachers, superintendents, principals, parents, and school board members who have contributed valuable insights and best practices to this work. We honored many of them in the second edition, which was released in 2014, and we hope to honor more of them in this third edition.[2] Their voices are found throughout these pages.

If you have read either of the first two editions, you will find that this third edition has a familiar feel. The leadership principles and strategies remain much the same. However, this edition is filled with a library of new stories, updated research, and fresh best practices. We believe you will find it invigorating and full of promise for today's young people.

So welcome to the third edition of *The Leader in Me*. We trust you will be inspired.

Sean Covey
Muriel Summers
David K. Hatch, PhD
leaderinme.org

1

Rippling Across the World

This chapter tells the story of *Leader in Me*: how it started, some of the places it has gone, some of the outcomes it has achieved, and why it is so relevant and important in today's reality. Most importantly, it tells of the impact it is having in individuals' lives—for students and for adults.

As you journey through these pages, we encourage you to study them with the mind of an educator and the heart of a parent. Does what you are reading make practical sense to implement in a school? Would you want your child to enjoy these types of outcomes?

We begin in North Carolina, where Dr. John Shepard faced a decision. Like many high school principals, he had a pay incentive in his contract based on academic success. The better his school's test scores, the better his pay. Focusing on anything other than academics had the potential to cost him some extra dollars, yet he knew his students needed more than academic preparations if they were to launch successfully into life the day after graduation.

Without regard to what it might cost him personally, Dr. Shepard did what he felt was best for his students. He and his administrative team set aside time twice each week for an advisory period. They called it LEAD time. It was time dedicated for students to set goals, learn leadership skills, and prepare for their future in the workforce.

Initially, students resisted. "Why are we doing this?" they asked. Before long, however, students were asking for LEAD time to be expanded. "This is about us," they said. "We want more time for these discussions!"

Dr. Shepard did extend the time allotted, and his school is now nine years into *Leader in Me*. Was the risk worth it?

"The school culture has significantly improved," says Dr. Shepard. "Students are happier. Teachers and staff are happier. Students are learning how to solve real-life problems. And several former students return each year to express gratitude for what *Leader in Me* has done for their lives beyond high school."

But what about the academics? In short, the academic improvements have been as profound as the cultural improvements. For the past few years, the school has consistently scored in the top ten high schools in the state in terms of student academic growth, and that is with approximately 50 percent of its students being English as a second language learners.

In Texas, an assistant principal reflected on what *Leader in Me* has done at her school. "The leadership skills contained in *Leader in Me*," she said, "were exactly what our students needed to prepare them to handle difficult life situations. But the reality is that *Leader in Me* was exactly what our staff needed. It has given them the boost they needed for our school to turn things around. And, in all honesty, the *7 Habits* have been just as timely for me and my life."

In New York, the 2,200 students at the Leonardo Da Vinci Intermediate School 61 represent over 100 nationalities. The staff knew it needed something to unite its students. One of the teachers, Antonella Caccioppoli, read *The Leader in Me* and approached Principal Joseph Lisa to say, "I think this could possibly help us." Mr. Lisa read the book and felt it was worth further investigation. So he presented the idea to the staff and their initial reaction was one of hesitation: "How can we possibly take on one more thing?" Mr. Lisa was sympathetic to their feelings yet knew something needed to be done for the sake of the students. So he said, "Let's at least start by having conversations and testing some of the ideas with a few teachers and students."

After the entire staff went through training in *The 7 Habits of Highly Effective People*, some teachers began having conversations with students about the habits. The teachers found that the habits were benefiting students and providing a common language to use in the classroom. They were further pleased to hear that the habits were trickling into students' homes and benefiting parents as well. It was not long before the entire school was implementing *Leader in Me* and involving the parents. They now insist, "This is not 'one more thing.' It is a central part of who we are and how we operate within our school."

In the Republic School District, located in Republic, Missouri, Superintendent Dr. Matthew Pearce was facing a familiar challenge: Academic performance across the district's seven schools wasn't where it needed to be. Serving just over 5,300 students, Republic's school performance data painted a mixed picture. While some schools were performing in the 70s—with scores of 71 percent, 74 percent, and 78 percent—others lagged behind, with two schools hovering around 52 percent and 53 percent and two more just reaching 60 percent. Something had to change.

Dr. Pearce had tried the conventional approach—leading with academics—but soon realized that instruction alone wasn't enough to move the needle. "First and foremost," he explained, "our leadership team, including myself, had to grow in our understanding that leadership is not just about academic achievement—it's also about culture and leadership. No district is going to exceed the capacity of its leaders."

This realization prompted a shift. The district began intentionally focusing on culture, implementing *Leader in Me* and using the Measurable Results Assessment (an assessment that is part of the *Leader in Me* process) to track progress. For the first time, they had metrics to give equal weight to leadership and culture alongside academics. That clarity opened the door to systemwide improvement. "We had been working in silos," Pearce said. "Once we started using *Leader in Me* and *The 4 Disciplines of Execution* (4DX), it all clicked. Our school improvement plans started aligning with our strategic plan. It was no longer double work—it was integrated work."

The impact was real. Employees began reporting greater satisfaction, and families felt more engaged in and connected to the school. Elementary schools—previously seen as trailing behind the secondary level—surged forward, with Schofield Elementary standing out as a remarkable example. Once one of the lower-performing schools in the district, Schofield is now consistently at the top.

Academic performance in the district soared as a whole and every school made improvement, with six of the seven making dramatic improvements over a period of just a few years. By focusing on the entire ecosystem and not just academics alone, they were able to achieve the kind of academic improvements most districts dream of.

Reflecting on this transformation, Dr. Pearce shared, "The *Leader in Me* framework is the plate—it's the thing that holds everything else. The nice thing about this framework is that you can use the plate and you don't have to put too much else on there, because it's an all-encompassing school improvement, student leadership, student culture, adult leadership, adult culture piece that can make a school a great place to be."

Also in Missouri, the Fort Zumwalt district administrators and school board were intent on providing students with the workforce readiness skills they needed to succeed in the world. Their students were doing relatively well with their academics, but they lacked some basic skills for getting along with others, such as conflict management and communication. In fact, they were at a point where the administrators felt that the only way they could raise their academic scores was to improve the cultures of their schools. They felt they could do that by improving the social and life skills of their students.

At the same time, teachers in the district were in need of a spark, something to reenergize their passion for teaching. So the district began providing *7 Habits* training for the staff in five of its elementary schools, followed by *Leader in Me* trainings in leadership, culture, and academics. Things went well enough in those initial five schools that all twenty-six schools in the district have since been trained in the habits and are now implementing *Leader in Me*. District superintendent Dr. Paul Myers says that "*Leader in Me* has changed the way students and adults function within our schools. Teachers are eager to teach the *7 Habits* to students and to give them real leadership roles and responsibilities. They feel they are making a difference in students' lives. They feel they are doing what parents and the community want for their children."

Fort Zumwalt School District leaders know how important it is that, as a Tier 1 system of support, all students be taught and equipped in applying the *7 Habits* in their daily lives. They continue to apply the principles and practices of the *Leader in Me* process to improve academics all throughout the district.

In Panama, one *Leader in Me* school operates in a red zone, a dangerous neighborhood. Many of its students live with either a single parent or grandparents, as did eleven-year-old Arturo.

Arturo's father had just been let out of jail, and his mother was still in custody when his father enrolled him and his younger brother and sister at the school. Arturo had been expelled from four previous schools, and it didn't take long for him to let the other students at his new school know who he was. Any excuse was a good excuse to hit the first student who crossed his path. His respect for teachers was no better.

One morning during arrival time, Arturo's little sister stumbled and fell. A boy bent down to help her, and that was all it took to enrage Arturo. He tackled the boy and started hitting him. A few classmates quickly intervened. They begged Arturo to calm down.

The classmates told Arturo that he could not continue to behave in this way. They explained that this school was a different type of school. They told him about the *7 Habits* and why, when he feels the urge to react, he must first pause and think about what he is going to do. They explained that all students at the school were friends and "no one looks for fights. We only want to help each other."

For Arturo, those words were foreign to how he had learned to behave his whole life. From that day on, he began to live and apply what his classmates had taught him. After only three weeks, his father showed up at the school. "What has been done to my son?" he asked the principal. "He is a different child. I want to be taught the *7 Habits*. I want Arturo and his siblings to start having a real dad."

In Saudi Arabia, a group of professors from a top medical university contacted a local *Leader in Me* secondary school and asked if they could make a visit. Afterward, the professors revealed the reason for their interest in the school. They said that some of their university students had attended that school and that those students were more confident, more respectful, more ready to lead, and more prepared for the rigors of the university than were students from other schools. The professors wanted to see for themselves what the school was doing to prepare students. And following the visit, they further revealed that they were eager to enroll their own children.

In Australia, over 50 percent of Parktone Primary School's students had transferred out. Parents had lost confidence in the school. Teachers were dissatisfied. As Principal George Danson described it, "Our school was on the verge of closure and there was a sense of urgency to rethink our school." With the help of *Leader in Me*, they turned the school around. Enrollment quadrupled over a five-year period. But it was not until students began complaining to their parents during the breaks that they were missing school that the teachers truly realized that they were achieving something special. They had gone from being on the cusp of shutting down to elevating the lives of hundreds of students.

We could go on with more examples and more reasons why schools have embarked on their *Leader in Me* journeys. Similar stories are emerging out of all fifty states in the US and more than sixty countries. They are coming from Brazil, where more than fifteen hundred schools have adopted *Leader in Me*. They are arising from Pakistan, where more than five hundred schools are implementing this comprehensive school improvement process. They are coming from the Netherlands, the United Kingdom, Romania, and other parts of Europe. They are coming from Asia. They are coming from Mexico, Central America, and South America. They are coming from the Middle East and parts of Africa. Indeed, more than eight thousand schools worldwide are now applying the same leadership principles and research-based processes to their school cultures and academics.

In addition, schools and districts continue to adopt *Leader in Me* after learning about the evidence-based results *Leader in Me* has been delivering.

As a result of all this, *Leader in Me* continues to ripple across the globe in more districts, more schools, and more individual lives.

How It Began

So what is *Leader in Me*? What are the *7 Habits of Highly Effective People* and the *4 Disciplines of Execution*? And why are parents, educators, students, and community leaders saying, "This is important!"?

As with so many inspiring stories, the *Leader in Me* story has its beginnings with a series of influential teachers. We begin with Miss Rose.

Life was not easy when Muriel (a coauthor of this book) entered elementary school. She was raised in a small rural town, and her family faced all the usual ups and downs of life. The worst of the downs was when Muriel's father—whom she idolized—passed away. It greatly grieved her and left her mother alone to support her young family. If that was not enough to dishearten a young child, Muriel was placed in a classroom with a teacher who said things like, "You come from a small town. You will never be able to do anything of significance in this life. You might as well accept that now."

But then came fourth grade, when Muriel was fortunate to have Miss Rose as a teacher. Miss Rose was aptly named. Students blossomed under her nurturing. She said things like, "It is not so much what is in your bank account that matters, it is what is in your heart." She was a builder of students' self-confidence. She once told Muriel that she would make a great teacher one day, if that was what she desired.

Fast-forward several years, and guess where Muriel found herself? Standing in front of her first class of wiggly first-grade students and wondering, "Can I really do this?" Thankfully she remembered, "Miss Rose told me I could."

With time, Miss Rose's prediction came true. Muriel became a fine teacher and eventually a nationally and internationally recognized principal. To this day, she credits much of her success to the influence of Miss Rose and the confidence she instilled in all her students.

Who was a Miss Rose in your life?

Two Teachers Meet

About the same time Muriel was entering Miss Rose's class, a young man named Stephen Covey was entering the MBA program at Harvard University. His family was heavily involved in his grandfather's successful hotel business, and it was fully assumed that Stephen would join the business when he graduated. Yet when he returned home with his hard-earned, prestigious degree in hand, Stephen gently broke the news to his father: "Dad, I don't want to be a businessman. I want to be a teacher."

With his father's encouragement, Stephen went on to become a university professor. He loved teaching, and he loved interacting with students. Students responded so favorably to what he was teaching that his classes were moved to a campus arena that could hold hundreds of students. The topics he taught came from research he had conducted to discover what traits and behaviors highly successful people had in common. He eventually narrowed his findings to what he called the *7 Habits of Highly Effective People*.

Several of Dr. Covey's students went on to achieve prominent positions in renowned organizations. They never forgot Dr. Covey or his *7 Habits*. In fact, they frequently called on him to train their top executives in the habits. Eventually, after twenty-five years of teaching university students, Dr. Covey felt compelled to take the *7 Habits* to even larger audiences and even larger arenas. Before long, he was speaking in front of audiences of thousands and teaching top business, government, and education leaders all around the globe. Eventually, he captured the *7 Habits* in a book. That book has since sold more than forty million copies, and four decades later it remains at the top of bestseller lists all over the world. All the while, Dr. Covey never referred to himself in any way other than: "I'm a teacher."

Then came the day when Dr. Covey and Muriel met. At the time, Muriel was principal of A.B. Combs Elementary in North Carolina. It wasn't a bad school, but its academic scores were unimpressive and it was facing a real crisis. Enrollment had dropped by nearly half due to the aging population within its boundaries. They had tried to establish the school as a magnet school to attract students from beyond its boundaries, but the magnet it had selected was not working. The superintendent informed Muriel that her school needed to reinvent itself and come up with a more attractive magnet theme or it would be shut down.

But what could that new magnet theme possibly be?

About that same time, Muriel learned that Dr. Covey would be presenting the *7 Habits* at a regional seminar. She decided to attend. As she listened intently to Dr. Covey and his *7 Habits*, she couldn't help but feel how relevant the habits were to her personally. She also couldn't help but notice how absorbed the hundreds of other attendees were in listening to Dr. Covey and learning about the habits. That is when thoughts began to swirl in Muriel's mind.

By lunchtime, all Muriel could think about was: "Can these habits be taught to elementary students?" She got her courage up and approached Dr. Covey during a break. She asked if he thought the habits could be taught to students, even as young as kindergarteners. After giving it a moment's thought, he looked at Muriel and casually responded, "I don't see why not. Give it a try and let me know how it goes."

Leader in Me Is Launched

Muriel couldn't wait to get back to her school and her administrative team. She told them about the *7 Habits* and her experience with Dr. Covey. The more the team heard, the more they began to brainstorm ways they could weave the *7 Habits* into a new magnet theme.

In the process of their discussions, the team reached out to a few parents to ask what they wanted in a school. Of course, the parents wanted strong academics, but they also made it clear that they wanted their children to learn how to make friends and get along with others, how to work in teams, and how to develop a strong character ethic. They didn't want their children to be all brain with no skills for working with people. They wanted well-rounded children.

Some parents were business leaders. Their thoughts were mostly focused on students developing workforce readiness skills. One parent even handed Muriel a list of skills and traits that were most in demand in the business world. The list included:

* Communication skills
* Honesty/Integrity
* Analytical skills
* Interpersonal skills
* Initiative, to be self-starters
* Strong work ethic
* Teamwork skills
* Positive attitudes
* Organizational skills
* Creative minds[1]

The more Muriel and her team thought about the *7 Habits*, listened to parents, and considered what employers want, the more the word "leadership" kept entering their minds and conversations. It was not long before they exclaimed: "Let's have 'Leadership' be our school's new magnet theme!" As a school, they wrote and posted a new mission statement: "Building Leaders One Child at a Time." Muriel then approached her superintendent, who had threatened to shut her school down unless something changed. He was persuaded that the leadership magnet theme was a compelling idea and told Muriel to move forward.

With no instructions for how to create a leadership magnet, A.B. Combs created their own path and plan. That first year, one teacher per grade level volunteered to teach the *7 Habits* to students. One of the first things those teachers observed was that behavior problems declined in their classrooms. And when a behavioral issue did arise, the teachers found they could use the language of the *7 Habits* to solve or reduce the problem. Furthermore, the parents of students in the trial classrooms began reporting that their children were using the language of the habits at home. But what really caught the teachers' attention was that the test scores for the school edged up slightly that year, and that it was the students in the trial classrooms whose scores had made the difference. That was when the teachers agreed: "Every student deserves this!"

The following year, all teachers began teaching the *7 Habits*. They also started giving students opportunities to be leaders in their classrooms. They gave every student a data notebook where they could keep track of their goals, scores, and accomplishments. They brightened up their hallways with murals and quotes reinforcing their leadership theme. And soon their student enrollment had doubled, with hundreds of students on a waiting list. Over 40 percent of the students came from low-income households. Twenty percent spoke English as a second language and represented over forty nationalities. Discipline referrals dropped significantly. Parents were delighted, and many of them drove significant distances to have their child attend the school. Teachers were feeling renewed.

No, it didn't all happen overnight. It happened over time. But when A.B. Combs Elementary was named the number one magnet school of America just a few years after adopting the leadership theme, educators from all over

The media center at A.B. Combs Elementary invites all to remember the school's magnet theme—Leadership.

began calling and asking to visit. They wanted to know the process for replicating this leadership model. The reality, however, was that there was no established "process" for replicating the work at that time. That is when Muriel reached out to Dr. Covey to say: "We gave it a try as you suggested. Come see what has happened. It is exciting!" But what she was really saying was, "Stephen! We're trying to run a school, not a visitors' center and consulting business! We need your help!"

Dr. Covey did respond to Muriel's call for help, as did others from FranklinCovey Education, led by his son, Sean Covey. And today there is a process in place to replicate and expand on the process that was begun at A.B. Combs Elementary. We call it *Leader in Me* because it focuses on the leadership qualities that are within each individual—all students and all adults.

Secondary and Beyond

With the A.B. Combs story as context, it surprises many educators to learn that *Leader in Me* actually has its earliest roots at secondary levels.

Ten years after Dr. Covey published *The 7 Habits of Highly Effective People*, one of his sons, Sean, wrote *The 7 Habits of Highly Effective Teens*.[2] It featured the same *7 Habits* that top leaders around the world were being taught, but it was translated into teen-friendly terms with teen-friendly examples. It was simple and straightforward. Teens could read the book and quickly relate to each habit and apply it in personal ways.

As fast as FranklinCovey Education could create lesson plans to go along with *The 7 Habits of Highly Effective Teens*, secondary teachers began finding innovative ways to integrate the habits into whatever subject matter they were teaching. For example, one set of high school teachers integrated the *7 Habits* into the study materials for an English class that all freshmen were required to take. Students read the teen version of the book as one of their assigned readings and were challenged to blend the *7 Habits* into a variety of writing assignments. Another set of teachers at a different high school integrated the *7 Habits* into their sociology curriculum. They and their students looked for ways to apply the *7 Habits* to various social issues of the day. Another school taught the *7 Habits* as part of a course on leadership.

Regardless of where and how the *7 Habits* were being taught, secondary school students responded to the habits in powerful ways. For example, one student was filled with a venomous desire for revenge after his older brother was fatally stabbed during a fight. But then the young man was touched by a passage he read in *The 7 Habits of Highly Effective Teens*. It talked about Habit 2: Begin with the End in Mind, which emphasizes the benefits of living a purpose-filled life. He began to wonder, "What are my purposes in life going to be? Will they be to seek revenge and potentially end up in jail—or worse?" He wrote a poem and called it his personal mission statement. In it, he committed to devoting his life to doing good in honor of his brother.

At a tough inner-city high school, a student was assigned to read *The 7 Habits of Highly Effective Teens* as part of her literature class. She, too, wrote a mission statement. It consisted of a grand total of three words and an exclamation mark: "Never give up!" She intended those words to inspire her to become the first in her family to *go to* a university. She worked harder in school than she had ever worked before, and she went on to become not only the first in her family to attend a university, but the first to *graduate*.

While some secondary student successes do contain life-changing stories, far more common are the quiet stories of secondary students applying the habits in everyday ways, such as arriving to class on time or procrastinating on their homework less often. Or of students seeking to truly understand each other instead of focusing solely on trying to prove their points. Or of students making other relatively minor yet important life improvements.

That all being said, it was not until *The Leader in Me* book was released that secondary schools started looking seriously at the *7 Habits* as more than a set of skills to teach. They began seeing *Leader in Me* as a holistic process, not just for personal change but also for schoolwide transformation.

In many secondary schools, the demand for *Leader in Me* has come from students who have graduated from *Leader in Me* elementary schools. The only schooling they have experienced up to that point in their lives has been *Leader in Me* schooling, and they are surprised when they arrive at their secondary school to find that not every school does *Leader in Me*. They want to know: "Why isn't our school a leadership school?" "Why don't students have a voice in how things are done here?" "Why don't we set goals and use the *7 Habits*?" Before long, they set up meetings with their middle school principal to say, "We expected things to be different here. Can we talk about it?"

In many instances, middle school and high school principals report that they can actually tell which of their new students came from *Leader in Me* elementary and middle schools and which did not. Those from *Leader in Me* schools tend to be more respectful, take more initiative and responsibility, show a greater interest in the school, and have better people skills.

For other secondary schools, the draw to *Leader in Me* comes more out of necessity. Their school cultures are in disarray, and teachers, staff members, parents, and students are all saying: "We need to turn things around and head in a more positive direction!" In still other cases, it is the local businesses that are approaching secondary schools and saying, "These are the skills we want students to have when they enter the workforce, and we are not seeing them in our new hires. If we agree to sponsor it, would you be willing to teach the habits and other leadership skills to students?"

These are but a few of the reasons why *Leader in Me* has made its way into the secondary school level. And though it is beyond the scope of this book, we will briefly note that the *7 Habits* continue to be taught in numerous universities around the globe, which is right where Dr. Covey began teaching them at the beginning.

Make It Your Own

It is important to note that elementary and secondary school teachers will typically take vastly different approaches to how they implement *Leader in Me*. This is due to differences in the maturity of their students and in how elementary and secondary schools are structured. For example, elementary school teachers typically have their students all day, whereas secondary school teachers are more likely to have students rotate in and out of their classrooms for an hour or so at a time. *Leader in Me* is designed to be adjusted for these differences.

In fact, regardless of grade level, it is expected that educators will adjust *Leader in Me* to match the needs and capabilities of their students and teachers. For example, if you hunger to enjoy a tasty hangi or want to learn the haka as part of a *Leader in Me* visit, then Western Heights Primary School in New Zealand is a great place to visit. The tamariki (students) and staff there love integrating and honoring its Maori heritage as a central part of their adaptation of *Leader in Me*. "We are not a clone of A.B. Combs," says Mr. Brent Griffin. "We do it the Whakaahu Way, our way. We built it around our strong connections to our Maori culture and four cultural principles: kotahitanga (unity), whanaugatanga (relationships), manakitanga (empathy), and rangati-ratanga (leadership)."

In other words, *Leader in Me* is not a cookie-cutter process. It is a set of powerful paradigms, principles, and practices that can be customized and adapted to any school in any culture in any part of the world. Needless to say, schools in Pakistan implement *Leader in Me* differently than schools in the Netherlands or schools in California. To use a chef analogy, *Leader in Me* is like a buffet of high-quality ingredients, and a school can cook them how they wish, spice them up as they see fit, and add their own ingredients to make their own delicious, organic, custom-made meal.

What Is Ahead

What you have just read contains only a small portion of the *Leader in Me* story. Much more is shared in the pages ahead.

This first chapter has described the early days of *Leader in Me* and provided a glimpse into why it is continuing to spread across the globe and at all grade levels. Chapter 2 will highlight the "why." Why are people saying *Leader in Me* is important and perfectly matched to the current reality? Chapters 3, 4, and 5 explain how *Leader in Me* is a process—not a program—and shares practical examples of how it is being implemented in schools and districts.

Chapters 6 and 7 share insights into how *Leader in Me* is engaging and benefiting families and communities. Chapter 8 suggests a model for how to launch *Leader in Me* and how to sustain it over time. Finally, Chapter 9 summarizes and reemphasizes the "why" of *Leader in Me* and concludes with a challenge for all adults who are in some way involved in preparing students for life beyond graduation.

We believe that as you progress through these pages you will find *Leader in Me* to contain numerous insights and perspectives that are timely and relevant for today's world.

Leader in Me encourages learners of all ages to embrace and enjoy timeless leadership principles.

2

Seeing, Doing, and Getting in New Ways

For some educators, *Leader in Me* feels like coming home. It is how they have always done—or wanted to do—things in a school. For others, *Leader in Me* feels more like a new shoe. It needs a little breaking in before it feels fully comfortable. And for others still, *Leader in Me* is a whole new way of seeing, doing, and getting.

But isn't that life? There are things we do that feel natural and things we do that require us to stretch our minds, expand our talents, and adapt to changing realities.

On the one hand, it can be argued that not much has changed in the field of education over the past few decades. Resource shortages, overcrowded classrooms, discipline issues, and so forth have been around for years. They are nothing new. On the other hand, "Wow! Things have changed!"

Indeed, much has changed in the past few decades that has forced educators to make adjustments to traditional ways of learning and teaching. Cell phones. Social media. Artificial intelligence. School violence. Anxiety. Loneliness. Depression. All these and more have brought new realities to schools and classrooms. Of course, not all these are entirely new. What is new, however, is the intensity and pace with which they are impacting students and are requiring teachers to *think* and *do* in new ways.

We use a simple model to provide a big-picture view of how *Leader in Me* works and how it helps educators adapt to changing realities. We call it the See-Do-Get Cycle, or the Change Cycle. It suggests that the way we "see" things in life (our paradigms) influences what we "do" (our behaviors and habits), which influences the results we "get" (what we achieve and become in life). The model assumes that if we desire to "get" different results than we are currently getting, then we need to change the way we "see" and "do" things, as illustrated below. Notice that the arrows in the model make a circle of movement. That is because *Leader in Me* is an ongoing cycle of continuous improvement.

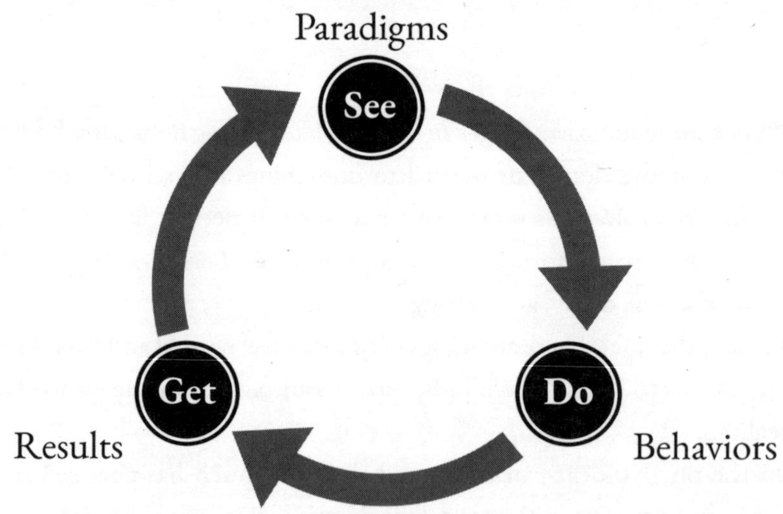

In this chapter, we first describe five paradigms that are core to *Leader in Me*. We then briefly introduce some of the best practices that *Leader in Me* teachers and administrators utilize—or "do"—to improve the lives and learning readiness of students. Last, we preview some of the promising results that are being achieved at *Leader in Me* schools and that will be further highlighted throughout the book.

What We "See"—Core Paradigms

Educators have many paradigms. A paradigm is a perception, a belief, or a lens through which we see the world. Educators have paradigms about themselves and about others. They have paradigms about how to teach and how to lead. They have paradigms about how to work with students, parents, and one another. They have paradigms about what is most important in a school and about what needs to change. Not all educators share the same paradigms.

Every significant *breakthrough* in life and in schools requires a *break with* old ways of thinking—old paradigms. This is called a paradigm shift. It is by shifting old paradigms to new paradigms that schools and individuals experience the most significant improvements.

Leader in Me embraces multiple paradigms. However, five paradigms are most core to *Leader in Me*. The five core paradigms are:

- The Paradigm of Leadership
- The Paradigm of Potential
- The Paradigm of Change
- The Paradigm of Motivation
- The Paradigm of Education

We will briefly describe each of these paradigms and contrast them with some of the more common paradigms that we encounter as we work with new schools. As you read about them, consider how they match with your present paradigms.

Paradigm of Leadership	
COMMON PARADIGM	**HIGHLY EFFECTIVE PARADIGM**
Leadership is for the few.	Everyone can be a leader.

A common paradigm in schools is that leadership is meant for the few. This is why the same small group of students always seems to be asked to be leaders in their school or classroom. Similarly, when asked to identify the adult leaders of a school, students, parents, teachers, and administrators are likely to point to the same small group of adults as being the leaders.

The reason people see the same few individuals as the leaders of a school is that leadership is often viewed as a position. The paradigm is that only the people who hold certain positions are designated as "the leaders." But according to Roland Barth, "A school should be a community of leaders—not just a principal and a lot of followers. The principal, teachers, students, and parents should all be first-class citizens of that community."[1]

With *Leader in Me*, the core paradigm of leadership is that everyone can be a leader. That includes all adults and all students. At a minimum, each person can be the leader of their own life. But each can also lead others toward achieving positive results without holding a specific title or position.

Over the years, we have enjoyed listening to elementary school students define leadership in their own words. One student said simply, "Being a leader is helping others." Another student defined leadership as "being good when no one is watching." Another insisted that one of his classmates was a leader because she helps him when he struggles in math. Another added, "I help little kids, so that's why I'm a leader." Another told his mother that he loves being a leader because it means "looking out for the underdog." With those definitions of leadership, why wouldn't every student and every adult in a school be considered a leader? They do not need to hold a position to do those things.

When participants in one of our corporate workshops were asked to name a person who greatly influenced their lives, one spoke up immediately: "It was the cafeteria lady at my elementary school," he said. "School was difficult for me. She was always there to ask how I was doing. She made me feel good about myself." We have heard equivalent remarks said about librarians, custodians, teacher aides, security staff, counselors, bus drivers, nurses, office staff members, and others. The official title of leader may not be in their job descriptions, but they were leaders nonetheless. That is what happens when leadership is not limited to a position.

A definition of leadership we frequently use with *Leader in Me* was one of Dr. Covey's favorites: "Leadership is communicating a person's worth and potential so clearly that they are inspired to see it in themselves." Again, with that definition, everyone can be a leader.

Paradigm of Potential	
COMMON PARADIGM	**HIGHLY EFFECTIVE PARADIGM**
A few people are gifted.	Everyone has genius.

A common paradigm in schools is that only a few people are gifted. In contrast, a core paradigm of *Leader in Me* is that everyone has genius in them.

The type of genius we are talking about is not based on a person being better or smarter than everyone else. Rather, it is based on every student and every adult in a school having unique perspectives, experiences, talents, and feelings that can contribute to the good of a school. It is the type of genius captured in Ralph Waldo Emerson's personal belief that every person he met was in some way his superior, and that there was something he could learn from them.[2] It is the type of genius first-grade teacher Pam Gil was talking about when she said, "I see every student as having gifts, and I might be the only person who can see those gifts in them. It is my job to reveal [those gifts] to them."

Muriel was approached one day by a parent of a new student at A.B. Combs. The parent was thrilled by what she had heard about the school but was worried about whether her son would be able to contribute. She asked, "Does my child have to be a strong leader to go to this school?" Muriel assured her that he would be able to contribute, noting: "This morning, a special-needs student, who has academic challenges, was assigned to welcome visitors to our school. He may not run a huge corporation one day, but he has interpersonal skills that make everyone feel happy and good about themselves. There will always be a role somewhere in our school for him. He feels so good about who he is in spite of his academic limitations."

Looking for the genius in every student—instead of the weakness—is a new

Taiwan students unite to celebrate their school becoming
a *Leader in Me* Lighthouse School.

way of thinking for some teachers. They are so accustomed to searching for
what is missing in students' academic abilities, or marking what is "wrong"
on exams or assignments, that it requires a real shift for them to focus first
on what students get "correct" or on what their strengths are and how those
strengths can be utilized to help students progress.

Students take great pride when teachers see their strengths and recognize
that they do have genius in them. The entire culture of a school changes and
synergy starts to occur as soon as people begin to view each other through
their strengths—their geniuses—not their weaknesses.

Paradigm of Change	
COMMON PARADIGM	**HIGHLY EFFECTIVE PARADIGM**
To improve schools, the system needs to change first.	Change starts with me.

We asked one teacher at a *Leader in Me* school, "If you could change one thing about your school culture, what would that one thing be?" She instantly responded, "Me."

Yes, change may be necessary and inevitable in life and in schools, but when the word "change" is brought up in so many discussions at schools, it is usually done within the context of "The school system needs to change." Or "Students need to change." In contrast, a core paradigm of *Leader in Me* is "Change starts with me."

A paradigm that holds that the "system" must change before a school can improve is often a reactive paradigm. It means waiting for others to act before one chooses to act, whereas a paradigm of "Change starts with me" is a proactive approach to change. It means looking inside one's self and saying, "There are things I can change in myself right now without waiting on others." It is the belief that "By improving myself, I am improving the school." Clearly, there will always be things about the system that need to change, but the best place to start is with what you can directly influence—yourself.

During a multicultural event, students celebrate the universal spirit of *Leader in Me*.

Schools do not behave—people do. And that is why school culture will change only when individuals change. It is an inside-out process. "Too many leaders prefer to take an outside-in approach," says Principal Brett Shelby. "They spend their energy blaming others or trying to get everyone else to change before working on themselves."

When one school was about to start implementing *Leader in Me*, the teachers were in the midst of joining teachers from other schools in protesting some of their district's policies. They were even threatening to go on strike. Not all the teachers, however, agreed on the best solutions. So there was not only tension between the teachers and the district, but there was tension among teachers. Yet as the teachers went through the *7 Habits* training, they slowly shifted toward a "Change starts with me" paradigm. In fact, they became so focused on the cultural changes they were making within their schools and their classrooms that they nearly forgot about their issues with the district.

Whenever the culture of a school is based on the paradigm that all the problems are "out there"—someone else's fault or someone else's problem to solve—that very paradigm may be what is keeping the school's culture and its students from progressing to their upmost potential.

Paradigm of Motivation	
COMMON PARADIGM	**HIGHLY EFFECTIVE PARADIGM**
Direct and control student learning.	Empower students to lead their own learning.

A major objective of education is to empower students to eventually graduate and lead their own lives—as much as possible. That includes enabling them to lead their own learning.

Many schools and classrooms are overmanaged and underled. In too many cases, administrators and teachers are so focused on doing their utmost to direct and keep tight control over all that occurs in their school or classroom that they struggle to find time or energy to be leaders. Words like "direct" and "control" are management words, whereas words like "empower" and "entrust" are leadership words. While management and leadership are both important in schools and classrooms, the most effective administrators and teachers learn to lead people and manage things. People who are led learn how to become self-sufficient. People who are managed don't.

Too often, teachers and administrators start a new school year with a leadership paradigm, but it doesn't stick. They are excited to inspire students and open their minds to new ways of thinking. These are leadership qualities. But then the new year gets underway and a few of the students start acting out during class. With good intentions, some teachers shift into management mode. They start trying to direct and control everything students do. Any thought of empowering or leading students goes away. The teachers may pride themselves in maintaining a sense of order, but in the end, the best it will produce in students is compliance. It will seldom inspire any form of lasting change in students.

One problem with a direct-and-control style of classroom management is that there is always a set of students who actually like a lot of rules. "Tell me exactly what you want me to do," they think, "and I'll do exactly as I am told so I will get a top grade." That way, the students don't need to think or plan on their own, since the teacher does the thinking and planning for them. That is not empowerment. And when it comes time to graduate, the students will sadly realize that there is no longer someone to tell them exactly what to think or do. They will lack the ability to lead their own learning and risk failing to launch successfully into society.

For students to become empowered to lead their own learning, part of the ownership for their learning must always remain with them.

Paradigm of Education	
COMMON PARADIGM	**HIGHLY EFFECTIVE PARADIGM**
Educators focus solely on academic achievement.	Educators and families partner to develop the whole child.

From the origin of schools, the primary role of educators has been to address students' academic needs. To educate their minds.

Yet it is no secret that when students show up to school hungry, sleepless, sick, not feeling safe, or otherwise not having their *physical* needs met, it is difficult to focus their attention on learning. And when they show up feeling anxious, lonely, depressed, angry, or otherwise not having their *emotional* needs met, it is again a challenge to get them fully ready to learn. Therefore, the luxury of focusing solely on students' academic needs is seldom matched to reality.

For these reasons, educators recognize the need to address the whole student—mind, body, heart, and spirit. As Muriel puts it, "If we are putting all of our efforts onto the almighty test score alone, I am quite afraid that we

Core paradigms provide the foundation for what inspires
educators and students at *Leader in Me* schools.

are going to create a generation of children who know how to do nothing but take a test well."

The *Leader in Me* core paradigm promotes educating the whole child. It strives to introduce students not only to the basics of reading, writing, math, science, history, and technology but also exposes them to the world of art, music, sports, business, world cultures, social well-being, physical fitness, and so forth. Furthermore, it suggests ways that educators can benefit from partnering with parents for the long-term good of the whole student. This is why the remaining core paradigm—the paradigm of education—partners educators and parents in developing students who are well-rounded, whole-person leaders of their own lives.

These are brief introductions to the five core paradigms of *Leader in Me*. All five core paradigms play essential roles in improving the culture of a school and preparing students to launch successfully into today's and tomorrow's realities. They are also instrumental in enabling educators to address the following three challenges that are common to educators.

Our experience is that unless schools truly strive to implement these core paradigms, it will be hard to create significant change of any kind. Everything begins with our paradigms, how we see and interpret the world. As Dr. Covey used to always say, "If you want to make minor changes, change your behaviors, but if you want to make quantum, significant changes, change your paradigms." Schools that implement *Leader in Me* with fidelity are schools who adopt these paradigms. Students can feel when a teacher truly believes that they have genius, that they can be a leader, and that they are loved.

What We "Do"—Addressing Three Challenges

Leader in Me and the five core paradigms will not solve every challenge educators encounter. However, what *Leader in Me* does do is apply its vast library of leadership principles and tools to addressing three challenges that all educators face. The three challenges deal with leadership, culture, and academics.

The three challenges are often viewed as separate. Yet the reality is that they interact with and impact one another. For example, recall that when A.B. Combs began teaching the *7 Habits* (leadership skills) to its staff and students, they saw simultaneous improvements in students' behaviors (culture), as well as progress in test scores (academics). So by directly addressing one of the three challenges, they were indirectly impacting the other two. This is why we depict the three challenges in the form of an interactive Venn diagram, as illustrated below.

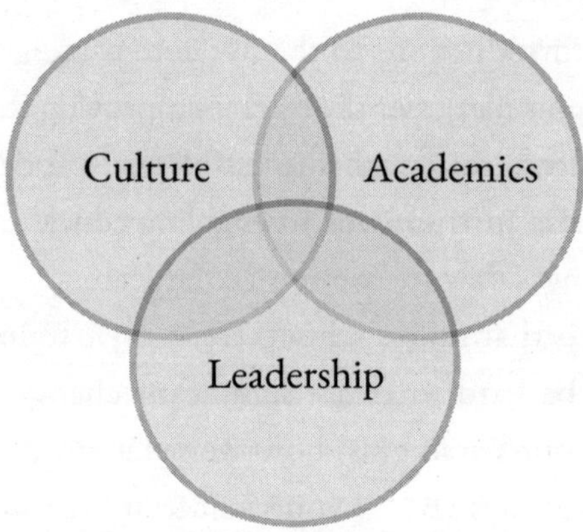

For each of the three challenges, *Leader in Me* focuses on two leveraged areas of improvement—two things that educators can "do" to improve their school and students' readiness to learn. What follows are brief descriptions of the three challenges and their leveraged areas of improvement. More detailed explanations follow in Chapters 3, 4, and 5.

Leadership

Leader in Me teaches leadership skills to adults and students. The leadership skills all come from FranklinCovey's vast library of leadership content and world-class training. They can be applied to individuals, teams, schools, districts, and families. They contain many of the workforce and life readiness skills that businesses and parents want for their children. Since everyone in a school is viewed as a leader, the leadership skills are taught to adults and students alike.

Start With Adults Learning and Modeling. The obvious reason for teaching leadership skills, including the *7 Habits*, to adults is to ensure teachers understand them enough to teach and model them for students. However, the *7 Habits* and other leadership skills that are taught as part of *Leader in Me* are just as beneficial for adults as they are for students.

Indeed, many adults in *Leader in Me* schools report improvements in their abilities to lead their own lives and to lead others, including their families. They talk about the habits not so much as a curriculum, but as a way of thinking and as something that has changed their lives. This is why adults being trained in the *7 Habits* are told, "Forget about your students during this training. This is about you. This is a gift for you."

Teach Students to Lead. Once the adults in a school are trained in the *7 Habits*, teachers are eager to teach them to students. That is timely because local businesses these days are pleading for educators to provide students with relevant workforce readiness skills. They want students to exit school with communication skills, teamwork skills, time management skills, conflict management skills, conceptual thinking skills, listening skills, organizational skills, and so forth. They desire students who embody such traits as integrity, empathy, honesty, initiative, optimism, and a strong work ethic. Each of these skills and traits is contained in the *7 Habits* and other leadership concepts encapsulated in *Leader in Me*.

But the question that often arises is: Can students as young as four years old really learn to apply the *7 Habits* and other leadership skills? That is the same question Muriel asked Dr. Covey when they first met. And what Muriel and her teachers have proven over the past twenty-five years is that, yes, even very young students can learn and apply the habits. In fact, many students learn the habits far better than most adults who attend workshops.

Why? Because for students it is not just a workshop. They are gradually drip-fed and reminded of the habits over a period of months and years. It is not a onetime event. Students hear adults using the language and modeling the behaviors, which reinforces student learning. It is a daily process of actively learning and applying the habits. Additionally, unlike the adults, students don't have as much to unlearn, and can pick up and apply the *7 Habits* principles more easily.

Culture

In many instances, school administrators allow the creation of a school culture to become a passive, "just let it happen" endeavor. Whereas what is needed to sustain a vibrant, engaging culture is a proactive approach, an intentional plan to improve and sustain a highly effective school culture.

Two things *Leader in Me* educators "do" to improve their school cultures are to create a positive leadership environment and to share leadership responsibilities with all adults and all students.

Create a Leadership Environment. What school in today's reality is not dealing with disengaged students or chronic absenteeism? And what school is not seeing pockets of declining teacher engagement or other challenges related to the overall culture of their school?

A positive school culture is not built by happenstance. It is built by intentional design. That is why *Leader in Me* is proactive when it comes to creating a physical environment that inspires students and a social and emotional environment that is nurturing, welcoming, and offers engaging schoolwide events.

Share Leadership. In *Leader in Me* schools, all students and all adults are given opportunities to be leaders, whether in their classrooms or in roles throughout the school. This does not require them to hold a formal leadership position. What it does require is for students to be given voice and choice in what happens in the school, particularly with regard to how they fulfill their leadership roles. Giving them an assignment and then telling them exactly what they must do is not giving them an opportunity to lead. That does not empower them to lead. *Leader in Me* is designed to give students a chance to take ownership of their leadership responsibilities by letting them decide how best to take charge of the responsibilities they are given.

Academics

While *Leader in Me* does not provide strategies for teaching math, reading, science, or other standard academic subject matters, what it does "do" is enable educators and students to be more focused in their academic endeavors. Two ways this happens is through teaching them how to set and achieve "Wildly Important" academic goals, and through empowering them with teaching strategies and tools that inspire them to take more ownership of their learning.

Achieve Goals. One of the best ways for students to take ownership of their learning is to set academic goals that are specific and achievable. To do this, they and their teachers are taught the leadership skills found in *The 4 Disciplines of Execution for Educators*.[3] They are the same *4 Disciplines* that top business leaders utilize to improve their organizations' productivity and outcomes. Each of the *4 Disciplines* is explained in detail in Chapter 5.

Empower Learners. If being able to memorize facts—facts that are now on students' phones—is no longer the great differentiator between students who succeed in the new reality and those who do not, what, then, is the great differentiator? It is possessing above-average creativity, strong problem-solving skills, and a knack for foresight. It is also having strong critical thinking skills and knowing how to analyze, optimize, synthesize, present, and do worthwhile things with facts. All this can happen when students are empowered with the leadership skills and tools that will allow them to take more effective ownership for their learning. Some tools include leadership portfolios that enable students to track their progress, student-led conferences that put them in charge of sharing their growth and areas of targeted improvement, and teaching strategies that place ownership for learning on the students.

So there are three challenges *Leader in Me* addresses and two leveraged best practices for each challenge, as summarized in the table below. When starting out, *Leader in Me* schools do not try to implement all the best practices or address all three challenges at once. Rather, they follow a tailored process that enables them to integrate the best practices over time, at their own pace, and according to their specific needs and goals. They make it their own.

Leadership	Culture	Academics
Start with Adults Learning and Modeling	Creating a Leadership Environment	Achieve Goals
Teach Students to Lead	Share Leadership	Empower Learners

What We "Get"—Measurable Results

When a new teacher was hired at Dr. Bryan C. Jack Elementary, a Legacy School in Tyler, Texas, she brought her daughter with her. The daughter had struggled academically and socially at her previous school. She lacked confidence and was nervous about changing schools. Yet soon after arriving at the new school, the daughter began to perk up. This pleased the mother, who, as a teacher, was still getting acquainted with *Leader in Me*.

As the year progressed, things continued to go well for the daughter. So well that the mother was invited to speak at a conference about the impact that *Leader in Me* was having on her daughter. In preparation, the mother decided to get her daughter's view on the impact. She gave her phone to her daughter and sent her to another room to record her thoughts. With the camera recording, the daughter began to talk about setting goals and how her teacher talked with her regularly about her progress. She spoke about how she was excited to take the state exam. "I'm going to do my best to apply the strategies my teacher has taught me," she said. The daughter was joyful as she went on talking about her new school and the opportunities she had been given to be a leader.

When the mother viewed the video, she couldn't believe what she was seeing in comparison to her daughter's experience at her previous school. When the time for the state exams arrived, the daughter ended up passing one of two parts. She was delighted! It was the first time she had passed one of the parts. But she insisted, "Next year, I'm going to pass both parts."

Similar reports of the impact that *Leader in Me* has on students arise on a daily basis. Teachers also report impressive impacts on their lives. For example, with teacher engagement numbers declining and turnover rising, recruiting excellent new teachers has become a challenge for many schools. Yet *Leader in Me* principals often tell us about teachers from other schools approaching them about potential openings before any openings are even announced. They have heard about the school and want to be a part of the leadership model. One high school teacher told us recently about being offered a teaching position at a school that was closer to her home and offered higher pay. She didn't consider it for long. She loved the culture at her *Leader in Me* school, the attitudes of its students, her relationships with other teachers, and, particularly, the respect she felt from the administrators. She said she wouldn't trade her situation for the better commute or pay. Similar stories from other schools further illustrate why improved teacher retention is a common outcome of *Leader in Me*.

The outcomes and benefits of *Leader in Me* will differ for each school or district, since the reasons for implementing *Leader in Me* tend to be unique to each school or district. Whereas one school or district might use *Leader in Me* as a means to increase attendance, attendance may not be a matter of concern at another school or district. Some schools and districts view *Leader in Me* as a way to get academic impact, while others are primarily looking for culture impact. And some schools are just happy to report that their success indicators have remained flat while the numbers at neighboring schools have all trended downward. Many districts and schools see *Leader in Me* as simply their answer to providing students the workforce readiness skills they will need upon graduation. Some adopt *Leader in Me* as a holistic approach to leadership, culture, and academics. They see *Leader in Me* as their operating system aligned to their strategic framework and plan. Each year, they identify a significant gap area at the district level and use the *4 Disciplines of Execution* to close these gaps year over year.

While many positive results from *Leader in Me* are anecdotal, over one hundred independent studies in more than thirty countries have been completed that validate the efficacy and impact of *Leader in Me* on schools and districts. As well, at the time of this publication, 96 percent of these studies have been conducted within the last ten years, and 95 percent have undergone rigorous scientific standards and peer or committee review. A full and current list of these studies can be found at LeaderInMe.org, but here are a few highlights.

Leadership Impact

* Teacher Efficacy: Schools with robust leadership models saw up to 92 percent of teachers making more intentional instructional choices.[4]
* Student Agency: Over 95 percent of surveyed teachers at *Leader in Me* schools report improved student leadership abilities.[5]
* Student Behavior: *Leader in Me* schools report 42 percent fewer behavior incidents.[6]

Culture Impact

* Attendance and Behavior: Schools reported a 45 percent increase in overall school attendance and a 90 percent reduction in discipline incidents over five years.[7]
* Family and Community Engagement: 83 percent of principals note improved parent satisfaction, enhancing the support network around each student.[8]

- Safe and Welcoming: 89 percent of teachers surveyed describe their *Leader in Me* school as safe and welcoming, promoting trust and emotional security.[9]

Academic Impact

- ELA and Math: A large-scale study reports a 6.7 percent increase in ELA performance and significant math improvements compared to pre–*Leader in Me* performance.[10]
- Better High School GPAs: A study of ninth graders found 91 percent of *Leader in Me* students earned a GPA of C or better, compared to 75 percent at non–*Leader in Me* schools.[11]
- Long-Term Impact: Secondary school students in *Leader in Me* schools achieved 17 percent greater academic success compared to those in non–*Leader in Me* schools, with *Leader in Me*–based instructional strategies positively impacting students across various proficiency levels.[12]

Overall Impact

In a meta-analysis using twelve studies that encompassed 198,176 students and 522 teachers, it was found that *Leader in Me* had a significant positive impact on:

- School Climate
- Student Behavior
- Student Attendance[13]

Those are just a few highlights, and the stories of impact are growing by the day. In one such example, a team of researchers from the University of Missouri recently conducted a study about four *Leader in Me* elementary schools. All four schools had been implementing *Leader in Me* for at least four years. They were selected due to differences in their demographics and reasons for implementing *Leader in Me*. They included an urban school where half the students were English as a second language learners. That school implemented *Leader in Me* as an attempt to address high student turnover rates, low academic achievement, and challenging student behaviors. A second school was in a rural, low socioeconomic status area that had recently seen a significant influx of higher socioeconomic status families. That school adopted *Leader in Me* to strengthen their small community. A third school, located in a prosperous middle-class suburb, was strong in academics but lacking emphasis on the emotional well-being of their students. The fourth school was attended by students from a wide range of socioeconomic backgrounds, and it adopted *Leader in Me* to accommodate its high proportion of special-needs students. So clearly, the four schools were different types of schools and had different reasons for implementing *Leader in Me*.

Though the four schools differed in their demographics and purposes, the results from interviews conducted with teachers, students, principals, and parents were similar. They reported that as a result of *Leader in Me* implementation, teachers became more prosocial, used more effective discipline strategies, developed better relationships with students, felt more camaraderie with one another, and found teaching easier and more enjoyable. As for students, the research indicated that they became more prosocial, engaged in less bullying or problem behaviors, developed greater confidence, and became more motivated, harder-working, and self-regulated learners. Slight increases were also detected for achievement and attendance, and there were fewer disciplinary incidents for students overall. For low-socioeconomic-status students or those students who previously disliked school, the positive effect of *Leader in Me* was at times dramatic.

Much of the change reported at these schools was rooted in the role students were playing as leaders. One teacher noted, "The biggest difference between us and a non–*Leader in Me* school is that students run the show. They've taken a lot off my plate." Another teacher agreed, saying, "The biggest change resulting from *Leader in Me* is that the students are more empowered now. Before *Leader in Me*, we had a school where the teachers were in charge and the students did exactly what their teachers said to do. But what we are seeing now is students taking on leadership roles and more collaboration happening between the adults and students. It's been a huge change." A parent added, "They let the children lead. The kids are confident. I've never seen kids between the ages of kindergarten and fifth grade get up in front of a room full of adults and speak the way they do." A number of teachers reported that their school had become a place where teachers wanted to be.[14] These outcomes are consistent with outcomes at other *Leader in Me* schools that have implemented the process with fidelity.

Since schools approach *Leader in Me* for varying reasons, it is convenient that they are able to measure and track their unique outcomes and progress with the Measurable Results Assessment (MRA), which is a standard part of *Leader in Me*. It draws feedback from a variety of stakeholders, including students, staff, and parents, and it is recommended that schools collect that feedback at least twice a year.

Look for similar results from schools, districts, and individuals throughout the book. Most of the outcomes—what schools "get" as a result of *Leader in Me* implementation—fall under one of the three challenges that *Leader in Me* attempts to address. The general outcomes are described in the table below.

Leadership	Culture	Academics
Highly effective students and adults who are leaders in their school and community	A high-trust school culture where every person's voice is heard and their potential is affirmed	Engaged students who are equipped to achieve and entrusted to lead their own learning

Putting It All Together

What we have briefly overviewed in this chapter are five core paradigms (what we "see"), three challenges *Leader in Me* addresses (what we "do"), and some basic outcomes (what we "get") that might be expected for schools that fully implement the *Leader in Me* process. Together, these components begin to unveil an overview of what we refer to as the *Leader in Me* framework. It is a continuous effort toward whole-school, whole-student improvement.

The A.B. Combs teachers and staff have been implementing the framework and process for more than twenty-five years, and they are still finding innovative ways to improve their efforts and systems and to adapt them to the changing world of education and the changing needs of students. One thing the A.B. Combs staff has done extremely well is to remember that the ultimate ends in mind of *Leader in Me* are not about teaching leadership skills, are not about creating a school culture, and are not about improving academics. Those are means to greater ends.

The greater ends in mind are for students to develop the skills and mindsets that will enable them to become self-sufficient, to be independent leaders of their own lives. They are for students to be able to work interdependently and effectively with others. They are for students to make meaningful contributions wherever they go in life—at home, at school, at work, and at play. As one principal said it, "We are producing successful humans, not just successful fifth graders." And it happens over time, not just over one year of a student's life.

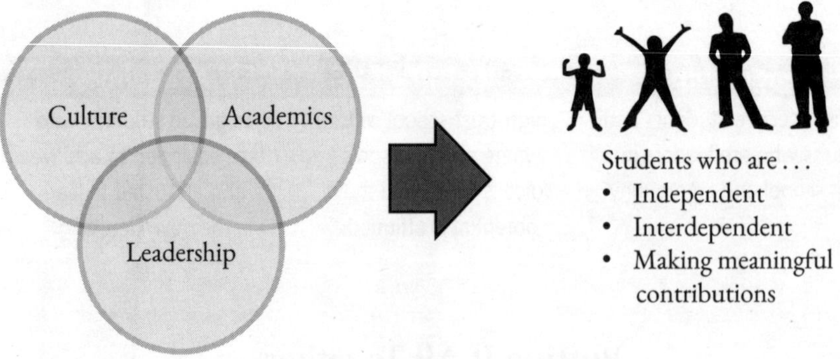

Perhaps the most important end in mind is for every student to know that their individual worth is of more value than any score on any test or any grade on any assignment.

It is important to note that these same ends in mind also apply to every adult in every school. After all, one of the primary reasons *Leader in Me* gets such great outcomes is because it takes an inside-out approach, meaning it starts with the adults in the school before going to the students. *Leader in Me* is as much about the adults in the school as it is the students. If we can first equip and empower the adults with the leadership paradigms, principles, and practices they need, they will in turn model and teach these to their students. Isn't it silly to think that we can change a school by getting the students to change first? In reality, the key is to get the adults to change first and to then model that change for the students. It's inside-out, not outside-in.

Roland Barth, the founding director of the Principals' Center at Harvard University, put it this way: "The nature of the relationships among the adults who inhabit a school has more to do with its quality and character and the accomplishments of its pupils than any other factor." How profound is that? In other words, if you want to have a great school and get great outcomes with

A teacher applauds the leadership, respect, and collaboration demonstrated by students.

your students, make sure that the adults in the school get along. Make sure those relationships are high-quality and the culture, the feeling, that come from that will permeate throughout the school. The students will feel it, the parents will feel it—everyone will feel it. And this will lead to positive results. This is why *Leader in Me* starts with teaching leadership skills to adults. It's the only place it can start.

3

Teaching Leadership Principles

As a university professor, Dr. Covey wanted to identify the attributes that lead people to be "most successful." So he researched hundreds of leadership books, journal articles, and biographies of inspiring individuals. From that research came his classic book, *The 7 Habits of Highly Effective People*.

Dr. Covey never claimed to have invented the habits. Instead, he insisted that the *7 Habits* are based on timeless, universal principles. The principles have existed for centuries and apply to all people regardless of their age, background, or where they live in the world.

For four decades, millions of individuals and top leaders around the world have been applying the *7 Habits* to enhance their personal effectiveness and the productivity of their organizations. Two of those top leaders are Peggy and Andrew Cherng, founders of the highly successful Panda Express restaurant chain. From their company's earliest beginnings, the Cherngs built the culture and values of their organization on essentially the same principles that are contained in the *7 Habits*. So when they learned that educators were teaching the *7 Habits* to elementary students, they wanted to see for themselves.

Mr. Cherng was first to visit A.B. Combs. He was astounded by the students' knowledge of the *7 Habits* and their ability to use various leadership tools. So, toward the end of his visit, he met with a group of students and gave them his sincerest praise. In the process, a third-grade student raised his hand and asked: "Mr. Cherng, we appreciate the praise, but what do you see as some of our deltas?" In other words, do you have any advice for how we can improve our school?

Mr. Cherng was stunned. He was amazed that a third-grade student even knew what a delta was, let alone that he and the other students were asking for advice on how to improve their school. They were talking as if they were part of the school's administrative team. And in a very real sense, they were. That is because at A.B. Combs everyone is learning how to be leaders.

The 7 Habits of Highly Effective People

So what are the *7 Habits*? And how is it that students as young as four and five years old can describe the habits better than many adults?

Perhaps Arlene Kai, a ten-year-old student from China, best described the *7 Habits* and their impact. "The *7 Habits* are like vitamins," she said. "You're healthier, happier, and more successful when they are a daily part of your life." As you glance through the following brief descriptions, ponder: Would a person be "healthier, happier, and more successful" if they applied the *7 Habits* in their daily life?

Habit 1: Be Proactive ("I am in charge of me.")

- I take initiative to act on life rather than waiting for life to act on me.
- I choose my actions, attitudes, and moods.
- I focus on what I can control, not on what I cannot control.
- I do not blame others for my mistakes or wrong choices.

Habit 2: Begin with the End in Mind ("I have a plan.")

- I know what is most important in my life.
- I have a personal mission statement.

- I know where I want to be with my life in five years.
- I plan ahead and set goals.

Habit 3: Put First Things First ("I do what's most important first.")

- I spend sufficient time doing the things that matter most in my life.
- I schedule my priorities and then stick with my schedule.
- I say no to distractions or things that I know are a waste of time.
- I am organized with my time and resources.

Habit 4: Think Win-Win ("Everyone can win.")

- I balance courage for getting what I want with consideration for what others want.
- I go for win-win outcomes with others, not win-lose, lose-win, or lose-lose.
- I make deposits in other people's Emotional Bank Accounts.
- I look for solutions to conflicts that benefit all sides.

Habit 5: Seek First to Understand, Then to Be Understood ("I listen first.")

- I try to see things from others' viewpoints.
- I listen to others without interrupting.
- I diagnose problems before I prescribe solutions.
- I voice my ideas and feelings with confidence.

Habit 6: Synergize ("Together is better.")

- I value other people's strengths and learn from them.
- I work well with people who think different from me.
- I do not insist that my ideas are always best.
- I brainstorm well with others and let the best idea win.
- I seek out other people's ideas to solve problems or plan events.

Habit 7: Sharpen the Saw ("Balance is best.")

- I take care of my body by eating healthy, exercising, and getting sleep.
- I spend quality time with my family and friends.
- I consider myself a lifelong learner.
- I find ways to bring meaning to my life.

Sometimes the best way to experience the power of the *7 Habits* is to think about living life according to their opposites. For example, consider what it would be like to live life based on the *7 Habits of Highly Ineffective People*:

- Be Reactive—just let life happen and get angry when it doesn't favor you.
- Begin with Nothing in Mind—never plan or think ahead.
- Put Last Things First—fill your life with time wasters.
- Think Win-Lose—win at the expense of others.
- Seek First to Be Understood—talk first and talk a lot and then pretend to listen.
- Go It Alone in Life—your ideas are always the best ideas anyway.
- Burn Yourself Out—never take time to renew yourself.

Some people say the *7 Habits* are just common sense. That may be true. But common sense is not always common practice. Living the *7 Habits* is not a onetime event. It is an ongoing process of continuous improvement.

While each habit stands alone as a powerful concept, each also builds on the others. That is because there is a sequence to the habits. For example, applying Habit 3, Put First Things First, requires that a person knows what "first things" are, which is what Habit 2, Begin with the End in Mind, is about. And how does a person begin with the end in mind if that person does not first feel they can act on life, which is what Habit 1, Be Proactive, is about? So you can see how the first three habits follow a natural sequence—first Habit 1, then Habit 2, and then Habit 3.

The first three habits—Be Proactive, Begin with the End in Mind, and Put First Things First—enable individuals to become more *independent* and self-sustaining individuals. Effectively applying all three of these habits leads to what Dr. Covey called the "Private Victory," or victory over self.

The next three habits—Think Win-Win, Seek First to Understand, then to Be Understood, and Synergize—enable individuals to be more *inter-dependent*. We live in an interdependent world. People need one another. So it is important that students learn how to work together and benefit from each other's strengths. These three habits lead to what Dr. Covey called the "Public Victory."

According to Dr. Covey, the Private Victory precedes the Public Victory. To be effective with others, first be effective personally. It is similar to what happens on a commercial airplane when passengers are instructed in an emergency to put on their own oxygen mask prior to helping others. People who are unstable personally have a difficult time strengthening others.

Even the walls cheerfully teach the basic principles of the *7 Habits*.

Habit 7, Sharpen the Saw, sustains and enhances each of the first six habits. It focuses on the principles of renewal, life balance, and continuous improvement. It strengthens the "whole person" by keeping a person fit in four areas—body, mind, heart, and spirit. The more a person sharpens all four saws, the more proactive they can be, the more choices they will have when beginning with the end in mind, the more disciplined they will be in putting first things first, and so forth. So Habit 7 truly does support and strengthen all the other habits.

In examining the brief summaries of the *7 Habits*, perhaps you noticed that they contain many of the same traits and workforce readiness skills that parents and business leaders want their children to be taught in preparation for life and entering the workforce. (See the table below—"Bringing the *7 Habits* to Life.") You may have also noticed that the *7 Habits* apply as much to adults as they do to students.

The 7 Habits	What Parents and Business Leaders Want for Students
Habits 1–3	**Independence (Private Victory)**
Be Proactive	Initiative, Responsibility
Begin with the End in Mind	Planning, Goal Setting, Vision
Put First Things First	Time Management, Organization, Integrity
Habits 4–6	**Interdependence (Public Victory)**
Think Win-Win	Conflict Management, Courage to Stand Up for Self, Consideration for Others, Ethical Living
Seek First to Understand, then to Be Understood	Listening Skills, Empathy, Public Speaking Skills
Synergize	Teamwork, Decision-Making, Openness, Humility, Respecting and Valuing Differences
Habit 7	**Continuous Improvement**
Sharpen the Saw *Care for Body, Heart, Mind, and Spirit (the whole person)*	Physical Wellness, Love for Learning, Emotional Wellness, Meaningful Service

Start with Adults Learning and Modeling

Highly effective schools have one thing in common—highly effective educators. And that is why the *Leader in Me* process begins with teaching *The 7 Habits of Highly Effective People* to the adults in a school.

Indeed, the *7 Habits* are as much for the benefit of the adults as they are for students. When a first-year teacher in Iowa was asked what the habits had done to improve her school, she instantly identified a few examples: "They have helped me to become less reactive to students, to become more organized with my class time, and to listen more effectively to parents. Today, I responded calmly to a situation involving a student, whereas prior to learning the habits, I would have reacted in anger." Notice how each of the improvements this teacher saw in her school was actually a self-improvement. She went on, "I don't just need to be teaching students how to be proactive, I need to be modeling how to be proactive."

Consider another example. After two years of implementing *Leader in Me*, a teacher wrote to us: "The *7 Habits* have had a profound impact on my life. I had come to believe that I had arrived at the upper limit of my potential, and that I didn't have anything more to learn or to give. Today, I am not the same person I was two years ago. I believe in myself more. I am trying new and creative approaches to teaching. And I am living with a renewed conviction that as a teacher I am contributing an important service to my community."

Still another example comes from one of the largest school districts in the United States, where a *7 Habits* workshop was held for principals. Near the conclusion of the workshop, the group was joined by the superintendent. He listened for a short time and then paused the workshop to ask the principals, "How would you describe the training you have received these past two days?" One principal's hand shot up immediately. "I've been attending professional development trainings in this district for thirty years," he said. "This is the first time one of the trainings has been about me rather than about some new policy, curriculum, or program. This has already inspired me to make changes in my life. I wish I'd had this thirty years ago. Thank you for making this available." Other participants spoke in agreement. They felt honored to be receiving the same quality training that top leaders around the world were receiving.

For as powerful as the *7 Habits* can be for adults, it is tempting for some to hear the habits and think: "I have some students who really need these habits." Or, "My spouse needs these habits!" Or, "I hope my colleagues are listening." Yes, some adults may think such thoughts. But one of the very first things they are told at the beginning of any *7 Habits* workshop is: "Forget the students for now! This is not about your spouse or your peers! This is about *you*! This is about applying the habits to your personal and professional life." In other words, it is an inside-out process. Start with yourself, then influence others.

The *7 Habits* are but one portion of a bigger process. For that process to be effective, there needs to be a team that holds the primary responsibility for developing an implementation plan that fits the readiness and goals of the school. That team includes the principal and a *Leader in Me* coordinator at a school level, as well as a district coordinator if it is part of a district plan.

Principal & Coordinator Training

Leader in Me utilizes a team to design and coordinate an overall implementation plan. That team is referred to as the adult lighthouse team. One of the team's greatest responsibilities is to involve everyone in the school in the planning and implementation process, rather than doing it all alone. Remember, everyone has genius, and everyone can be a leader.

The lighthouse team creates smaller action teams that are empowered to plan and carry out specific portions of *Leader in Me*. It coordinates plans and schedules to prevent various action teams from duplicating efforts and to avoid overburdening people. It ensures that all *Leader in Me* efforts are focused on achieving the school's highest priorities.

The principal is an important part of the lighthouse team but can delegate much of the responsibility for coordinating the overall *Leader in Me* plan to a coordinator. Additional adults are also invited to participate on the team, based on their talents, interests, availability, and roles. They meet with a coach who facilitates the process at the beginning and at various milestones, with the understanding that each school's plan will be unique.

New and Ongoing Staff Learning

One of the lighthouse team's earliest responsibilities will be to plan for when and how the adults will be trained in the *7 Habits.*

A typical approach to getting the adults trained in the *7 Habits* is to offer a workshop to the full staff prior to a new school year, though it can happen in the middle of a year or whenever professional development opportunities are available. The training is facilitated either by a FranklinCovey coach or a certified coach from a district. One important benefit of the adults going through the *7 Habits* training together is the bonding that takes place during the various discussions and activities.

For adults who join the staff after the workshop, they are encouraged to read or listen to *The 7 Habits of Highly Effective People* book, or to complete a self-paced version of the habits online, and to attend a regular *7 Habits* workshop at its nearest availability.

To keep the *7 Habits* fresh and to deepen the staff's understanding of them, it is important to create opportunities for the adults to receive ongoing "boosters." Some schools, for example, provide their staff with a morning message every Monday that is focused on one portion of one habit. Other schools encourage grade-level teams to discuss the *7 Habits* topics that are most relevant to them or their students. Many schools do a back-to-school booster for the staff at the beginning of a year to refresh everyone's overall understanding of the habits and to share new ways to apply them. It is important that the discussions focus on the adults applying the habits, not just the students.

In addition to the *7 Habits,* there are additional leadership skills and insights integral to *Leader in Me.* They include such world-class resources as *The 8th Habit* and *Teacher Believed in Me* (introduced in Chapter 4), *The 4 Disciplines of Execution for Educators* (introduced in Chapter 5), and *The 4 Essential Roles of Leadership* (introduced in Chapter 8).[1] These, too, are taught to top leaders around the world, and are important to the *Leader in Me* process. They are taught at various milestones in the process. We provide glimpses into what these content areas entail in the coming chapters.

Family and Community Partnerships

Leader in Me does not minimize the roles that parents, guardians, and community leaders play in a school's overall levels of achievement. Therefore, training opportunities are also made available to them. They can be invited to participate in trainings alongside the educators, or separate workshops can be held, such as *The 7 Habits of Highly Effective Families* workshop. Involving families and community leaders is so important to the process that we have dedicated entire chapter discussions to them in Chapter 6: Bringing It Home and Chapter 7: Engaging the Community.

Teach Students to Lead

Decades ago, it could almost be assumed that students would learn at home the life skills and character traits that are found in the *7 Habits*. But as an assistant superintendent pointed out to teachers in her district, "Students don't always arrive at school with these skills. So why leave it to chance whether or not they learn these skills? Why not level the playing field and give every student the opportunity to learn these habits?"

The *Leader in Me* approach to teaching the *7 Habits* to students involves more than a stand-alone curriculum. It integrates the habits throughout a school day and in a variety of ways. But let's start with describing how the *7 Habits* and other leadership skills are taught through direct lessons.

Direct Lessons

Teaching direct lessons is a common way to start the process of students learning the *7 Habits* and other leadership principles. A typical approach is to focus the first days of school on providing students with an overview of the habits, one habit per day. The *Leader in Me* contains a whole library of preK–12 direct lessons that can be taught at various lengths. They are designed by teachers, for teachers, and use all types of instructional strategies to make the learning engaging and to accommodate different learning styles. There is ample opportunity for teachers to add relevant stories, games, manipulatives, movies, poetry, contests, art projects, and so forth to make the lessons more tailored to specific students. Teachers are experts at making the lessons their own.

One first-grade teacher, for example, turns her classroom into a leadership camp for the first two weeks of school. She sets up a large tent in the classroom and adds various decorations to create a camping environment. As students enter for the first day of school, their full attention is set on figuring out what that tent is all about. The teacher then facilitates outdoor activities that teach the habits. Students love her camp and emerge with a basic understanding of each habit and what it means to be a leader.

At secondary levels, plans are also plentiful for direct lessons. However, it is common to engage the students in composing songs, writing raps, or replacing the lyrics of popular songs with clever *7 Habits* messages. They learn as they create. We have been amazed at what students produce and how much they enjoy figuring out ways to apply the lessons. That being said, secondary teachers have great stories to tell and strategies to use for connecting the habits with students and in ways that no scripted lesson can. So, between what students provide and what teachers craft, masterful lessons occur.

Numerous teachers find student-friendly clips from the internet that teach or illustrate one or more of the *7 Habits* or other leadership principles. Once students see a few video examples that their teacher finds, they begin finding examples of their own. Better yet, they make their own videos that teach a leadership principle. At one high school, they had a media class that year after year consistently had only ten to twelve registered students. One year, the students in that class were asked to create videos that supported the *7 Habits*, and those videos were shown to the whole school during morning announcements. The next year, the class was filled to capacity, and a second section of the class was added. Why? Because students had seen the videos the previous year and wanted to be able to make videos and have their videos shown to the whole school.

A number of teachers work with their classes to create and perform skits as a way of learning and relearning the habits. A teacher in Florida created a trail mix recipe that had seven ingredients. Each ingredient represented one of the habits. Many teachers simply take existing activities they have done for years with students, and they tweak them ever so slightly to incorporate one or more of the habits.

These are but a few creative ways we have seen teachers teaching the habits using direct lessons. There appears to be no end to their innovation.

Numerous elementary teachers use *The 7 Habits of Happy Kids* to get students started with the habits.[2] Written by Sean Covey, it uses fun-filled character illustrations and takes a chapter-per-habit approach to teaching the habits to young students. The illustrations capture K–6 students' imaginations and allow them to quickly acquire the language of the habits. At secondary levels, *The 7 Habits of Highly Effective Teens* or even *The 7 Habits of Highly Effective College Students* can be used as text resources for students to learn the habits. The intent is to keep the direct lessons short and engaging, and to drip-feed them to students throughout the school year.

In cases where secondary students have been enrolled in *Leader in Me*

School mission statements cross borders to welcome and guide all who walk the halls.

schools from the early grades and are well acquainted with the *7 Habits*, then the emphasis at secondary levels might be placed more on learning and applying other leadership skills and traits. In fact, the *7 Habits* are only part of the library of lesson plans. This is particularly true at secondary levels, where students are focused on developing the workforce and university readiness skills they will need upon graduation. Many states and countries have developed Portraits of Graduates that contain lists of the skillsets and character traits they believe to be essential for students. *Leader in Me* offers a comprehensive Student Leadership Portrait that covers personal leadership, interpersonal leadership, team leadership, and organizational leadership. It is supported by a carefully focused curriculum filled with numerous topics and modules that include:

- Living the *7 Habits*
- Achieving Goals
- Strengthening Wellness
- Finding Your Voice
- Developing High Trust Relationships
- Contributing to the Community
- Succeeding with People
- Leading Teams

Students don't just learn about leadership as part of the eight modules—they prove they can lead. They are given opportunity to earn micro-credentials that show they can apply the principles found in the modules and that students can put on their résumés and university transcripts.

So, there are plenty of topics and lesson plans for teaching students the habits and other leadership principles. The question that always arises is, "When?" When might teachers find time to teach the *7 Habits* given all the other things they teach?

The answer to that question will depend on the teacher and the school. Many schools already have dedicated time first thing in the morning when they hold class meetings. Some call this time LEAD time, advisory, homeroom, class meetings, academies, or some fun name connected to the school's mascot, like Tiger Time. They devote ten to thirty minutes to teaching the *7 Habits* and discussing other school interests, such as morning announcements.

Globally, more and more countries are mandating that schools set aside time for such leadership and workforce readiness lessons. They have listened to parents, business leaders, and fellow educators, and now require that such skills be taught for a minimum of one hour each week. A number of *Leader in Me* schools in these countries have chosen to dedicate that one hour to teaching the *7 Habits*.

Numerous high schools have created semester- or year-long courses that teach the *7 Habits* and other leadership skills in greater depth. Much of their time is dedicated to applying the leadership skills through hands-on leadership projects.

For students who are new to an already existing *Leader in Me* school, it can be a surprise to show up to school on the first day and hear the language of the *7 Habits* being spoken. They might think it is a foreign language. So, several schools have created "bridge" training for new students. This entails a series of short lessons that introduce the new students to the language, paradigms, and excitement of *Leader in Me*. For example, at A.B. Combs, the school counselor, Sam Woodrum, teaches a class for new students (and new staff) that he calls Combs 101. It covers the basics of the *7 Habits* and *Leader in Me* so that new students and teachers are not so surprised by what they see or hear during their first days at the school.

As with anything, there are things to be cautious about when teaching the habits. For one, it can be easily overdone. Students have multiple years to learn the habits, so they do not need to be taught all habits at once or every day. Second, the habits should not be used as words of punishment. If all that students hear of the *7 Habits* is "Why were you not proactive?" or "You need to put first things first!" or "You must learn to seek first to understand!" chances are they will be steered away from—not toward—the habits.

One of the most important keys to successfully teaching leadership principles is consistency. Make it a habit. At Mountainville Academy in Utah (a K–6 elementary school that has been successfully implementing *Leader in Me* for over a decade), every classroom spends the first fifteen minutes of each day doing a leadership lesson from the *Leader in Me* curriculum. But it wasn't always that way. The principal of the school said, "I used to tell my teachers that they could do 'leadership time' anytime they chose, but that often led to inconsistency, and teachers often waited until the end of the day to do it and then ran out of time. Knowing how important leadership was to us, we decided to make it the first part of every day in every classroom. This has been a game changer for us. We are all on the same page now and it's strengthened our leadership focus and increased our teachers' ability to teach and model leadership themselves."

Integrated Approaches

The ideal is for the *7 Habits* to be taught *somewhere* and *everywhere*. "Somewhere" refers to the direct lessons and having dedicated leadership time. "Everywhere" refers to finding ways to integrate the habits into most any subject matter lesson, assembly, newsletter, or other activity. It may happen in a planned manner or serendipitously.

A panel of students speak their voices as guests present them with questions.

Here's an example where the subject matter was science and the topic was seashells. It was a standard lesson that Mrs. Fowler had taught her second-grade students for many years. But this year, it was different. At the center of the lesson was a basket filled with seashells of all shapes, sizes, and colors. One by one, Mrs. Fowler plucked a shell from the basket and explained its parts and functions, the same way she had done it in years past. But then came a new twist. This time, prior to putting each shell back in the basket, Mrs. Fowler paused and pointed out a small nick, a little scratch, or some other minor flaw in the shell. When the final shell was put back in the basket, Mrs. Fowler whispered, "I have something special to tell you." The whispering caught her students' attention.

Mrs. Fowler explained that when she was in college, she developed a habit of pointing out other people's flaws, as she had done with the shells. She became particularly good at identifying the weaknesses of her roommates. Then one day an emergency arose. Mrs. Fowler desperately needed help. The only people she could think to call for help were her roommates. She called them one after another, and the only roommate to answer was the roommate with the most annoying flaws. Thankfully, that roommate came to her rescue and the emergency was resolved.

Mrs. Fowler told her students that from that point on she started to focus on that roommate's strengths instead of her flaws. In fact, the two became best friends. Mrs. Fowler said she learned from that experience that focusing on people's strengths instead of their flaws made her a happier person both in college and in life.

So, with a small adjustment, Mrs. Fowler had taken an existing science lesson and integrated a brief example on how to apply Habit 6: Synergize, which focuses on valuing others' strengths. It suddenly became one of her favorite lessons to teach.

Mrs. Johnson is a middle school teacher in Florida. She makes Habit 4: Think Win-Win part of her discussions on the earth's environment and the scarcity of natural resources. She asks students what will happen if people think only of their wants being satisfied without thinking about how others or future generations will be impacted. Students identify win-lose or lose-lose approaches to dealing with the environment and identify the consequences of those approaches. They then brainstorm win-win approaches.

Indeed, teachers at all grade levels insist that they can integrate one of the habits into just about any subject matter lesson or topic they teach. Sometimes it happens with a little bit of preparation; often it occurs serendipitously.

One of the simpler ways teachers integrate a habit into an existing lesson is through literature. That's because most books found on a classroom or library bookshelf contain stories or examples that apply one or more of the habits. Some teachers, for example, use *Alexander and the Terrible, Horrible, No Good, Very Bad Day* to teach about Habit 1: Be Proactive.[3] The class reads the book together and then students create skits to show how Alexander might more proactively handle the various "no good, very bad" situations he encounters. First, they act out possible reactive responses, and then they act out possible proactive responses. That is just one example of many books in which teachers find opportunities to illustrate and discuss one or more of the *7 Habits*. It helps when library specialists, such as Angie Headley, Lisa Ray, Erin Hardy, and so many others, actively look for books with *7 Habits* connections and share them as a service to teachers.

Writing assignments are another great way to have students make *7 Habits* connections. At a high school in Indonesia, for example, English teachers assign students books that tell stories about people who have faced tough decisions or circumstances in their lives. The students are then assigned to write short essays in the form of advice for how the featured individuals might have dealt with their situations using the *7 Habits*.

Another writing assignment is to have students write a personal mission statement. They can first read about Habit 2, which talks about personal mission statements, and consider what other students have written as mission statements, then they can write a mission statement of their own. Sean Covey includes multiple examples in *7 Habits of Highly Effective Teens* that students can look to for examples.

History lessons are packed with stories of leaders changing history by seeking first to understand or putting first things first. Teachers might ask students to read a chapter or story and then offer a discussion prompt like, "How might [name of a historical figure] have handled that situation more proactively?" Or, "How might that war have been prevented if the individuals had sought first to understand, then to be understood?"

Before retiring, art teacher Martha Bassett assigned several projects that had a leadership connection. A favorite was for fifth graders to design a front cover for *Time* magazine that included a self-portrait and a headline about something they might do in life that could someday land them on the cover of the magazine. While drawing pictures, students dreamed of future contributions they might make in their lives and the person they wanted to become.

Art assignments are a memorable way to motivate students to begin thinking about the future.

Music specialist Jacquie Wojtowicz integrates leadership principles and inspiring messages into just about every song her choir sings. It is no wonder that many students say hers is their favorite class. "Music teachers teach stu-

Students collaborate to bring leadership to life through artistic expression.

dents to sing, play instruments, and appreciate music. It's what they do," she says. "So why not choose and integrate music that is inspiring, uplifting, and reinforces positive character traits? It adds hope and positivity to students' days."

Jessica Hook has physical education students sharpen their saws and set and track goals for improving their exercise and daily fitness routines. She talks about synergizing when working in teams, and motivational quotes from sports figures hang from the walls of her gym. She touches students' hearts through more ways than aerobics.

Some subject matter topics may be more challenging to integrate with the habits. For example, it may not be simple for math teachers to integrate the habits into an advanced algebra lesson. However, they can invite students to synergize with one another when solving challenging problems. Similarly, technology lessons may involve having students design projects that require them to "begin with the end in mind" and to "seek first to understand." In fact, all teachers can say things to start a project or day, such as: "Our end in mind for today is to . . . ," or "Let me seek to understand what you are getting at when you say. . . ." Just hearing the language of the habits being used in real-life, practical situations can reinforce ways to apply the principles.

One of our favorite stories of how a teacher can integrate *7 Habits* lessons into their subject matter involves a high school teacher named Joe Gutmann. For years, he was a prosecuting attorney for the state of Kentucky. That role included sending teens to prison. While the intent, of course, was to keep communities safe, Joe couldn't shake the nagging feeling that he might make an even greater contribution if he was on the prevention side, keeping teens from getting into trouble in the first place.

Eventually, Joe made the proactive choice to give up his high pay and cushy office and become a teacher. He taught criminal justice at a high school located in a tough section of a large city. He was a longtime fan of the *7 Habits*, so he began telling his students about the habits and how they can be applied to life. In fact, if asked what subject matter he taught, he would smile and say, "I teach life."

Mr. Gutmann could weave the habits into any lesson topic he taught. The *7 Habits* language was a part of who he was and the language he spoke. Many of his students came from volatile home situations. Many had never met their fathers. They fully understood what Mr. Gutmann had given up to be with them, to be their teacher. Some saw him as the stable father figure they never had. So when he talked with them about life in his calm, assuring voice, his students listened.

As Joe neared retirement, former students lined up by the dozens to share how much he had influenced their lives. Many had gone to college thanks to his influence. Several had entered the field of law and criminal justice. And when asked to reflect back on his transition from attorney to teacher and whether he felt it was worth it, he replied humbly, "I used to be sending kids to jail. Now I am sending them to law school, to the Peace Corps, and to all types of positive professions in their communities. I couldn't be happier."

Indeed, there are many "everywhere" ways teachers can integrate lessons throughout their days and well beyond teaching the habits "somewhere" as a direct lesson. As Henry Duran, a secondary school teacher in Colombia, told us: "I just look for the teachable moments. When students start talking about issues that are heavy on their minds and I can see they are looking for resolution, I find ways to use the habits to help them work through the issues."

Service Learning

One of students' favorite ways to learn about leadership is through service learning. This is where emphasis is put on applying the habits and other leadership skills.

Pauline-Glenn Springs Elementary offers an excellent example of service learning. Each year, the administrators work with students to select a service learning project to pursue as a school. One year, the chosen service learning project was connected to the bestselling book *A Long Walk to Water*.[4] The book is based on the true stories of two eleven-year-olds in Sudan who make long trips to gather and haul water. One of them makes a two-hour trip twice a day to fetch water for her family. The students read the book and spend time throughout the year learning about where Sudan is on a map and some of its history, culture, and hardships. The students use their leadership skills to plan and raise the funds to drill two water wells in South Sudan. The fundraisers are all student-led.

Another year, the students chose a construction theme. They partnered with Habitat for Humanity, a not-for-profit organization that builds homes for families in need. The students were given chances to visit homes in development and see what it takes to build a home. As part of the process, they set goals for raising funds to contribute and used their goal-setting skills to track progress. Students came up with most of the fundraising ideas, such as making and selling bracelets and bookmarks. In total, they raised $20,000 by getting donations from people in the community. Each time they achieved a milestone, their principal, Jennifer Million, said the students would cheer for joy. She said, "It's not just talking about the habits, it's putting the habits in motion."

Pauline-Glenn Springs is just one of many schools with multiple service learning projects led by students. The Anderson Secondary School in Mexico City requires a service learning project for all senior students. Early in the school year, students identify about twenty service learning projects that they find interesting. Most have to do with service in the community, while a few are designed to benefit the school environment. Students then select which of the projects they want to participate in and work on planning their projects throughout the school year, with the help of parents, and raise funds if funds are needed. Some examples include planning a day's activity with a local care center for the elderly, working with an orphanage, helping with a humane shelter for stray animals, and building a flower garden area near the school's entrance. Much of the learning involves figuring out how to plan and how to work with others.

Generations School, the oldest school in Karachi, was among the first schools to adopt *Leader in Me* in Pakistan. They had a strong reputation for excellence and holistic education but wanted to build their culture into one that emphasized leadership, empowerment, and responsibility. This included providing opportunities for service learning. Students fully grasped the concept. Their Grade 4 students took the initiative to propose a full-day visit to Deaf Reach, a school for deaf students. According to the Generations School principal, Dr. Ghazala Siddiqui, "The activity was entirely conceived and led by students who wanted to serve the needs of the deaf students. The students organized fun activities to involve the deaf students, who they felt often get

Setting Wildly Important Goals helps students focus on
what matters most—personally and academically.

left out. It was a day not to be forgotten by adults and students. I felt so proud
seeing our students as empathic leaders."

One of the best ways for students to learn by serving is to assign them to
teach the *7 Habits* and other leadership skills to their peers or to younger
students. Secondary school students can be creative in preparing and teaching
the *7 Habits* to teach elementary school students. In preparing lessons, it is the
students doing the teaching who learn the most.

Again, it is important to note that in the process of doing service or setting
goals or completing projects, there are other leadership skills—well beyond the
7 Habits—students can develop that will be meaningful in their future lives. Not
the least of these are skills for setting goals, making plans, and public speaking.

Each year, for example, Colégio Anglo Morumbi, a K–12 Legacy School
in Brazil, involves students in selecting three schoolwide goals. One year, the
culture goal was to develop students' public speaking skills. They called it the

INSPIRE project. It was an opportunity for students to select a topic, prepare a presentation, and share it with their classmates in the form of a TED Talk. Manuela Righi, a fourth-grade student, shared her experience as follows:

> I was a very shy child. I was embarrassed to even say "good morning" to people. In class, I never asked questions or gave my opinion. I thought public speaking was impossible for me.
>
> But everything changed when our teacher, Patrícia, introduced the IN-SPIRE project. She explained that, to be a good leader, it was important to develop public speaking skills. She promised to teach us some techniques, but insisted that we also had to do our part, face our fears, and never give up. At the time, I thought: "I will never be able to do that!"
>
> As I watched my classmates take their turns speaking, I began to realize that each had their unique way of speaking. Some were more serious, others were more lively. There was no "right" way. I just needed to be myself, use the techniques I had learned, and trust my efforts.
>
> I learned to move around while I spoke, to maintain eye contact with people, and to vary my tone of voice to highlight the most important parts. I practiced a lot.

Not only did the school achieve its goal of teaching students public speaking, but Manuela did so well that she was asked to speak and share her story in front of a large audience of adults. She concluded by saying, "Today, I am here to say that if I was able to overcome my fears, you can, too."

The leadership skills Manuela learned in doing that project will benefit her throughout her life.

In Summary

In concluding this chapter, let us insert a reminder that the most effective way to teach leadership is by modeling. Not just "talking the talk" but "walking the walk."

Students will learn more from what staff members *do* than from what they *say*. It is the old adage "What you do speaks so loudly I cannot hear a word you say." This is also why the first step in the *Leader in Me* process is to get all adults in a school trained in the *7 Habits*. It is an inside-out approach. As adults exemplify the habits and other leadership skills, their lives become the best lesson plans for teaching students.

A secondary school principal in Utah stated, "If you're going to be teaching the *7 Habits* to secondary students, you've got to be living them. If not, teens will see the hypocrisy, and it will be next to impossible to get them to apply the habits themselves."

When it comes to modeling the habits, every adult in the school becomes a teacher. In a real sense, teaching begins with the front office staff. They are the first points of contact and the first impressions students and visitors encounter. The language they use and the way they treat people can help everyone learn, experience, and be reminded of the habits.

When teaching the leadership skills, *Leader in Me* teachers know how to make the habits age-appropriate, but they also know that they do not need to

Students greet their peers, actively creating a welcoming environment and modeling positive leadership behaviors at the start of the school day.

"water down" the habits. Trust that even the youngest students can learn the language of the habits.

When A.B. Combs first started teaching the habits at its school, many people were incredulous. "You can't teach the *7 Habits* to kindergarteners! The habits are for adults!" they would say. Until they began hearing students talk about the habits. They were amazed at what elementary school students knew and could apply about leadership. Indeed, even students at early learning centers have long since proven that teaching leadership to young students is not only doable—it is inspiring.

The *7 Habits* are now being taught around the world to students of all ages, from traditional public schools to private and charter schools. They are being taught at alternative schools and home schools. Students with special learning needs, such as autistic students or students with Down syndrome, tend to thrive on the common language of the habits and the structure that the habits and other leadership skills provide. Again, the *7 Habits* and other leadership skills are for all students. And all adults.

Learning and living the habits is a lifelong process. Dr. Covey himself, who lived the habits as well as anyone we have known, would talk about the habits he was striving to improve in his own life. One he often mentioned was seeking first to understand. Even though people who knew him would describe him as an excellent listener, he always felt he could do better. As you consider the habits, which habit do you consider to be a strength? It's important that you celebrate that strength and keep it as such. And which habit do you struggle with most? If you want to try to do better with the habits, that may be a good place to start. As Dr. Covey used to say when asked what the most important habit is, "The most important habit is the one you're having the most difficult time living."

In the end, the real reward is the number of students who return to the school and report life-changing results from having been taught leadership skills in their elementary and secondary school years. We are always personally thrilled to receive such anecdotal reports from students and teachers. And we receive hundreds of them a year. But we know that the real thrill is what happens when the educators and parents are able to witness firsthand the benefits that come to students in the form of skills and memories that will last a lifetime.

4

Creating a Leadership Culture

Whereas the previous chapter focused on teaching highly effective *habits*, this chapter focuses on creating a highly effective *habitat*—the school's culture. It is the type of culture wherein students like Lucy can thrive and capture a glimpse of who they want to become.

Lucy's middle school was early on in its *Leader in Me* journey. The administrators were determined to create a vibrant, inspiring learning experience from the moment students entered its doors. Someone suggested painting a large wall mural in a high-traffic area as a pleasant reminder of the *7 Habits*. Prior to *Leader in Me*, the immediate response would have been to think, "Let's hire a local artist to paint the mural" or "Let's get the art teacher to do it." But the *Leader in Me* paradigm is to first think, "What can a student do that an adult would typically be asked to do?"

When Principal Dr. Jill Scheulen, Assistant Principal Lance Wheeler, and school counselor Tara Beasley contemplated which of their students might be capable of painting such a mural, Tara spoke up. "What about Lucy?" Lucy was an eighth-grade student who had been diagnosed with a hearing impairment as an infant. Yet when it came to learning, her hearing impairment was less of a barrier than her self-worth impairment. It wasn't her study habits that kept her from becoming an above-average student—it was her lack of self-confidence.

Lucy was invited to paint the mural, and she chose spring break to perform the work. While other students were at the beaches and hanging out with friends, Lucy was at the school hanging out with her paintbrushes. And with each stroke, something special was being created. The mural portrayed the words "*7 Habits*," and each letter depicted a person dancing and celebrating the joy of living the habits.

When the other students returned from spring break, none could miss the new mural. It was brilliant. Everyone assumed it had been done by a professional. As word got out that Lucy was the artist behind the masterpiece, her peers were stunned. "The quiet girl who seldom says a word in class? How could it be?" they wondered.

People's perceptions of Lucy changed. More importantly, Lucy's perceptions of Lucy changed. She saw herself in a whole new light. No, her hearing impairment did not go away, but her self-worth impairment did. She told her mother, "Helen Keller had a hearing impairment and she was able to make important contributions, so I can, too."

Lucy was seeing her worth and potential in an entirely new light, and because of this, she began to communicate the worth and potential that she saw in others around her, including peers and even staff members. It was a ripple effect that permeated the entire school community.

The story does not end there. Lucy's success with the mural transferred to other aspects of her life, including academics. In what became a tribute to the administrators who trusted her and gave her the chance to express her voice through art, Lucy went on to high school and graduated top of her class. She earned a perfect score of 36 on the ACT and a perfect 800 on the math portion of the SAT. From there, she headed to Stanford, one of the most prestigious universities in the world, where she earned a master's degree in artificial intelligence.

The administrators could have instead provided Lucy with multiple months of academic tutoring or given her additional speech therapy, but would that have had the same impact on Lucy's academic progress as giving her the chance to find and share her voice?

Lucy and her mural showcase the *7 Habits* and the
genius within each person in the school.

The 8th Habit

People are often surprised to learn there is an 8th habit. Many students claim it as their favorite. What is it?

The 7 Habits are based on powerful principles that can be used for all kinds of purposes. In fact, the habits can even be used by thieves to plan and carry out a bank robbery. But using the habits for devious purposes, of course, was never Dr. Covey's intent.

"So, for what purposes are the *7 Habits* intended?" That was a question on Dr. Covey's mind when he suggested the 8th Habit. In fact, he suggested that the 8th Habit is not really one more habit, but rather an approach to using all *7 Habits* to pursue meaningful causes.

The 8th Habit is: Find Your Voice and Inspire Others to Find Theirs. Notice that there are two parts to the habit. One is to "find your voice," and the second is to "inspire others to find their voice." According to Dr. Covey, finding one's voice is a matter of self-leadership, leading one's own life, whereas inspiring others to find their voice is a matter of leading others. Finding one's own voice is typically accomplished by pondering and then acting on four thought-provoking questions:

> Talent: What are your strengths?
> Passion: What causes are you
> most passionate about?
> Need: What needs in the world do your talents
> and passions best address?
> Conscience: What do you feel good about
> doing?

Students proudly host guests from the community and put their leadership on display.

Where people's talents, passions, and consciences intersect with important needs in the world is where they will find their strongest sense of voice.

Once a person has found their voice, the *7 Habits* become powerful strategies for making their voice come to life. In that sense, the *7 Habits* become a *means* to a meaning-filled *end*.

Inspiring others to find their voice is a matter of leading others to find their voice. It does not mean to define for others what their voice will be, but rather to create conditions and opportunities in which they can find purpose in their lives.

The reason many students designate Habit 8 as their favorite habit is because there is a natural yearning within each person to make meaningful contributions. If that is so, then one of the greatest contributions teachers can make in students' lives is to give them opportunities to make meaningful contributions. In fact, it is often in the process of helping students find their voice that teachers find their own sense of purpose—their own voice.

This chapter is filled with best practices for how teachers can inspire students to find their voice by: 1) creating a leadership culture for the school, and 2) sharing responsibilities for leadership.

Creating a Leadership Culture

If students are taught highly "effective" habits and are then placed into a highly "defective" school culture—one that is unfriendly, unsafe, or where they do not feel valued—then those students cannot be expected to fully develop their newly learned habits. It is like taking a healthy seed, planting it in toxic soil, and expecting it to blossom to its full potential. Or as Principal Matt Thatcher describes it in education terms, "If you don't have the proper culture in place, nothing else, not even academics, will ever be what it needs to be."

So how do educators create a leadership culture?

A culture of appreciation and respect is nurtured by students at Pryor High School.

For starters, too many school administrators take a reactive approach to improving their school culture. They just let it evolve. They leap from crisis to crisis, putting out fire after fire. When problems like bullying arise or staff gossip sessions become the norm, they form a committee and make new rules to put out that fire (at least temporarily), and then wait for the next crisis to flare.

In contrast, *Leader in Me* educators take a proactive approach. They are intentional in designing a highly effective school culture in which students can learn and teachers can teach. Their culture is one where, as one teacher said to us, "people choose to be here because of the school climate that we have here. It has brought us all a lot closer together."

Building such a leadership culture includes creating an inspiring physical environment, establishing a welcoming social-emotional environment, and holding meaningful leadership events.

The Physical Environment

A principal in Singapore told us that there are three ways they teach leadership principles. One, by presenting lessons. Two, by modeling. Three, by what they place on their school walls. What messages do your school walls communicate?

The physical building at A.B. Combs has not changed since the day it opened. It remains the same fifty-year-old structure. From the outside it looks like most any other school. Step inside, however, and one can expect to discover a view that is not typically seen in a school.

On entering the front doors, students immediately see a colorful tile mural depicting the school's vision statement. Former fifth-grade students created it as a legacy gift. The main office to the left is so inviting that students want to be sent to the office. The ceiling tiles are decorated with self-portraits painted by teachers that depict them when they were in elementary school. They are a reminder of what it was like for them to be in elementary school.

Beyond the office is an intersection. To the left is a hallway with data charts

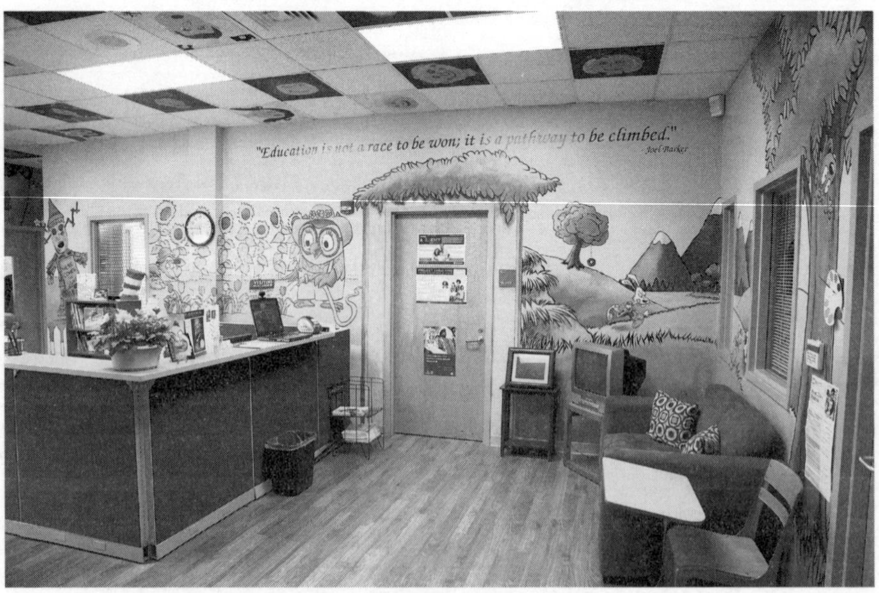

What students would not want to be sent to this office and
be greeted by the wall-to-ceiling joy of learning?

displaying academic progress. To the right are pieces of student art and photos of educators from around the world who have visited the school. Prominent for all to see is a sign that reads, "We honor the greatness in you."

And so it goes throughout the school's hallways. Each hallway is labeled with a street sign named after one of the *7 Habits* or some other leadership concept, such as Proactive Alley or Leadership Lane or Win-Win Boulevard. The kindergarten hallway is filled with bulletin boards connecting leadership concepts with academic learning. Each grade level has such a hallway, and each classroom has such a bulletin board. Most students have a piece of work on display somewhere in their grade-level hallway. The displays are refreshed regularly, making it feel as though the school is a living, evolving environment.

On several walls are quotations like, "Leadership is doing the right thing even when no one is looking." One hallway displays photos of students involved in fun school traditions. It is a memory lane. Another wall displays photos of community leaders—astronauts, dancers, artists, authors, etc.— who have visited the school and spoken with students about what it means to be a leader. In the cafeteria is a floor-to-ceiling painting that illustrates the *7 Habits*. A nearby hallway is lined with country flags to celebrate the various nationalities of students. Hanging high in the gym are motivational quotes related to athletics and teamwork.

Inside classrooms, the leadership theme continues. Walls are covered with science, math, vocabulary, and history displays, similar to what is found in most any classroom. Scattered among them are friendly reminders of the *7 Habits*, the class's goals, and student leadership roles. A class mission statement is placed in a prominent spot.

All in all, the entire building sends messages that say, "This is a place where you are seen, where you are heard, and where you are loved." The walls speak volumes to the students.

Similar physical environments appear in *Leader in Me* schools around the globe. While some displays are created by adults, the favorites are always those designed by students. Some displays are rotational, and they change frequently. Some are part of an annual theme. Others are meant to last with the thought of forever in mind; these are considered legacy displays.

While the "cutest" displays—including all kinds of misspellings and scribbled drawings—are typically found in the elementary school grades, some of the most impressive physical environments appear in secondary schools. By the time students reach secondary school, many have developed incredible talents. The walls are covered with artwork and displays of student achievements interspersed with inspiring quotations, as well as scoreboards, pictures of students working in the community and winning scholarships, posts of upcoming events made by classroom project managers, and recruitment flyers made by students for students. It is like visiting a student museum.

One particular display that captures the spirit of a *Leader in Me* physical environment at a secondary school is found at Swain County High School. The school has a tradition of excelling in sports, and for many years, both sides of the entrance were lined by a pair of glass trophy cases filled entirely with trophies from winning sports teams, some from decades long past. When students were asked what they wanted to see in the school's environment, one of the first things they mentioned was the trophy cases. They wanted the cases to be filled with the achievements of current students, and more than just athletes. It was decided that one section of the cases would be reserved to honor the most notable past and recent sports trophies, and that the rest would be filled with the accomplishments of current students from all aspects of the school. Those cases now display and celebrate students' achievements in all areas of academics, including STEM, art, home economics, woodworking, and so on. New achievements are added throughout the year.

One common best practice for schools is to create physical displays that highlight current students in high-traffic areas throughout the school, and then to reserve a special location to honor the students and accolades of the past. Pryor High School, for example, has set aside one section of a hallway where every past cohort of students has photos of its alumni on display, as if it is a living yearbook or photo journal that grows from year to year. Other schools create an alumni Hall of Fame to recognize individuals who have gone on to make noteworthy contributions.

A student-created mural prominently reinforces leadership
principles and adds sparkle to the school's environment.

The spirit of creating an inspiring physical environment was also captured when a visitor was being given a tour of a middle school in Missouri. The visitor noticed a long chain hanging from the ceiling of one hallway. It stretched from one end of the hall to the other. Each link in the chain was made of construction paper. Every student had made a link, and on it they had written their name and one of their strengths. The visitor noticed that the chain was hung low enough that most any student could either reach up or jump up and touch it. "How long has this chain been up?" the visitor couldn't help but ask. "Over a month," replied one of his student guides. "And no one has pulled it down?" asked the surprised visitor. The student guides seemed appalled by the question. "Why would someone tear it down?" they asked. "We made this. It represents that we are stronger when we work together." The look on their faces indicated that they couldn't imagine why the visitor would think someone would tear it down.

In some classrooms and schools, the walls look surprisingly bare at the start of the year. Then, day by day, display by display, students turn their classroom walls and school hallways into colorful places where students feel welcome. The goal of the physical environment is not to build an art museum—it is to build students.

Some schools create friendly spaces for students to socialize and study in groups. At an older high school in New York, for example, there was a small courtyard area that had been taken over by overgrown plants. It was an eyesore. One year, some students asked if they could fix it up, and soon they and other student volunteers had the area cleaned up, painted, decorated, and looking good. The courtyard quickly became a favorite place for students to hang out. Students feel ownership of that spot and are proud to say: "This place is ours. We created it."

At another high school, there was not sufficient space for students to socialize during times such as lunch. The adults discussed the matter, and with the librarian's approval they agreed to open up the library at lunchtime, not just for visiting but also for eating at the tables. The students knew that was not normal procedure and interpreted the gesture as a positive message from teachers and administrators: "We want you to socialize, and we trust you."

Some schools go out of their way to ensure that every student is represented in the physical environment. For example, at an intermediate school in Queens, New York, students represent over one hundred nationalities. To create a message of unity, each new student paints a tile that represents something about them and their cultural background. The tiles are then mounted all around the school hallways so that every student is represented. Following graduation, the students take their tiles home as a warm memory of their time at the school, and new tiles are put in their place once the new cohort of students arrives.

While the most popular displays tend to be those created by students, don't forget the creativity, artistry, and achievements of teachers and other staff. Why not highlight their talents and achievements, too? We have seen displays in schools that are filled with the work and achievements of teachers and other adults in the school. Some displays represent awards or achievements the staff have received, but a good number of them display the hobbies and handiworks of staff members that have nothing to do with the roles they fill in the school, including artwork, woodwork, and some priceless quilts.

In one New York City school, the security guard was an excellent artist, and she contributed to some of the school's best displays. Other schools mount uplifting quotes in the office area that are specifically intended to inspire adults, such as: "So many of my smiles begin with you." Or "In case no one told you today, you're a great teacher." One sign reads: "I teach tomorrow's leaders. I'm kind of a big deal." So when thinking of the physical environment, don't forget to honor and inspire the adults. What messages do your school walls communicate to them?

Additionally, *Leader in Me* schools will be full of publicly displayed scoreboards containing their Wildly Important Goals, which will be explained in greater detail in Chapter 5. Wildly Important Goals, or WIGs, are the vitally important goals that the school is trying to achieve. Schools typically have one WIG, and sometimes two, displayed near the main entrance of the building to quickly remind staff and students about the WIG they

Every school expresses leadership in their unique artful way; no two are fully alike.

are striving to achieve. Just like a scoreboard at a sporting event, publicly displayed scoreboards can generate strong engagement and rally everyone toward a common cause.

For example, upon entering Pontiac Elementary School in South Carolina, you'll encounter a five-by-ten-foot scoreboard posted near the school entrance that communicates the school's Wildly Important Goal. Classrooms will also post scoreboards for their individual classroom WIGs that are aligned with the overall school WIG, which are aligned with a district WIG for *Leader in Me* districts. Marshall Elementary has a large publicly displayed scoreboard that reads, "80% of all Marshall students will meet their monthly lead measure leadership goal." Such scoreboards are motivating for all and usually incorporate compelling goal achievement imagery that shows progress toward the goal, such as a thermometer, frogs hopping across a pond, cars racing to a finish, or hot-air balloons rising in the clouds toward their target.

When done proactively, thoughtfully, and with "leadership" in mind, a school's physical environment can be tremendously inspiring. As one parent told us: "The colorful physical environment and visual displays are evidence that teachers are invested in the school and care about students' experience." Or, as a teacher reported, "Our school is super inviting, with a warm atmosphere from the minute you walk inside the door. It impacts the students. I believe it also impacts the cheeriness of the teachers." And to those comments a principal added, "All of it is done with intentional purpose. If you see something on one of our walls, it has a meaningful purpose."

What intentional messages do your school's walls send to students and adults?

The Social-Emotional Environment

A school cannot change its culture merely by changing its physical environment. And while it is nice for walls to communicate students' worth and potential, it is even better when they *feel* it and *hear* it from an actual person.

When we asked Keli Sare, a principal in Florida, to describe the biggest difference *Leader in Me* has made at her school, she didn't hesitate to respond: "It feels different here." Meanwhile, a mother taking her son to school for the first day of kindergarten worried about how well he would do at the school. He had a lot of emotional issues. And yet she said that the minute she stepped into the school she totally relaxed. She hadn't even made it to her son's classroom, and she already knew he would be okay. "I could feel it," she said.

Indeed, when asked about what impact *Leader in Me* has had on their child, the top response from parents, by far, will be something like, "It has helped my child feel more confident." Many parents tell us how their child was struggling at one school and then moved to a *Leader in Me* school and ended up doing better socially and academically. They tell of their shy children coming out of their shell and being more social. They tell of their child not feeling bullied. They tell of their child feeling valued and appreciated.

One of our favorite stories of impact on a student occurred when a district assistant superintendent called a principal to ask if she and her teachers would consider enrolling a student named Devon. Devon lived outside the district's boundaries and had been turned down by other districts and principals who felt they could not properly support him. Why? Because Devon would never physically attend school due to extreme allergies. He would need to attend school via a robotic device—an avatar. A camera and screen on the avatar would allow him to view his class from home and allow his image to be viewed by his classmates. He could also converse with his classmates and teacher via the avatar. He could even direct the avatar to travel to various parts of the school. The principal and her teachers told the assistant superintendent that it would be a privilege to have Devon at their school. And it was. Students and staff all became friends with him via the avatar.

One of the best ways for students to feel welcome and valued in a school's social-emotional environment is to hear it. To have a teacher, administrator, or a peer tell them that they are welcome and valued. At Northwest High School in Cedar Hill, Missouri, they have an entire team of students dedicated to helping new students feel welcomed and valued. They call it Lion Crew. Their role is to look out for new students, to plan activities for new students, and to

From the moment students and guests enter a *Leader in Me* school they know there is something special happening.

be on the lookout for students who might be feeling lonely or isolated. They tell the new students in a variety of ways that they are welcomed and valued. They don't leave it to happenstance. It is a proactive approach with intentional plans and purposes.

Something students hear often in a *Leader in Me* school is the language of leadership. In fact, one of the most common benefits we hear about in *Leader in Me* schools is, "It gives us a common language." The *7 Habits* themselves are a major part of that common language. It happens as a natural outcome of teachers integrating *7 Habits* language into lessons, seeing it in hallway displays, hearing it during assemblies and meetings, and so forth. When hearing it spoken regularly, the students pick up the vocabulary of the habits in the same way they pick up the vocabulary of a foreign language or culture. They gradually become native speakers.

A great place and time for students to hear and pick up the *7 Habits* language is when teachers use the habits to praise students or give everyday instructions. "Good job being proactive, Sarah." "I love how you worked together and synergized in class." "I love how you were being a leader today, Anthony." "Our end in mind today is to get all ten spelling words correct." And so forth. Within just a few words, students will know exactly what the teacher is intending. As one teacher put it, "If I run into any student in the hallway—whether I know them or not, if they are misbehaving or are 'off-task,' I can say, 'Are you putting first things first?' and immediately the student knows what I mean. Even kindergartners."

One teacher noted how she uses the *7 Habits* to help students resolve conflicts: "If there is a disagreement happening between two students, I can say something like 'Let's seek first to understand each other,' and then I give each student time to explain their concerns. As soon as I say it, students know where I am going with the conversation and that they will have their turn to be heard. They immediately start to calm down." And the more students understand all *7 Habits*, the more they can be trusted to solve their own disagreements. Assistant Principal Brianna Welsh says that she also uses the *7 Habits* when mediating peer conflicts. She has the students turn to each other and then uses Habit 4: Think Win-Win; Habit 5: Seek First to Understand, then to Be Understood; and Habit 6: Synergize to come up with a solution to their conflict that fits everyone's best interests.

School counselors report similar benefits of having the *7 Habits* as part of their school's common language. School counselor Ashley Rich, for example, says that she uses Habit 1 "a lot" in her counseling with students. More specifically, she talks with them about what is in their circle of influence and what they can and cannot control. Julianne Sterbutzel, another school counselor, says, "I talk with students about carrying their own weather, and how they are in charge of how they choose to act. Or I talk with them about pushing the 'pause button' and to think before they act out of fear or anger." Julianne has even taken the *7 Habits* and aligned them with her state's resiliency standards so she can teach students how to use the *7 Habits* to build resiliency.

Not to be underestimated is when a central part of a school's culture and common language involves listening. Listening empathically, without judging students, communicates important information to students. It tells them that what they have to say is important. It tells them that they are important. It tells them, "I care about you."

Of course, what educators and counselors do not want to do is overuse the language of the habits or use it in negative ways. The intent is not to have a student get to their high school years only to shout from the rooftop, "If I hear the word 'paradigm' or hear a teacher say 'be proactive' or 'put first things first' one more time, I am absolutely going to freak out!" The *7 Habits* are meant to be used in temperate, positive ways. Students may even rebel against *7 Habits* language if it is overused or used as a tool of constant criticism: "Why are you so reactive?" "Why didn't you put first things first?"

The goal of building a positive social-emotional environment is to create a culture that nurtures and builds up students, that communicates their worth

Students express their leadership through art and through seeking first to understand.

and potential. Not a culture that is toxic and criticizes or tears them down. It is what adults want to experience as well.

Leadership Events

Leadership events are opportunities for students to apply their leadership skills, build a sense of community within the school and classrooms, and find and share their voice. Leadership events are also excellent opportunities to celebrate achievements. Favorite events can be turned into annual traditions.

Any typical school or classroom event—such as an assembly or awards ceremony, a parent night, field trip, concert, class meeting, school play, or sports competition—can be "leaderized" and turned into a leadership event. We share a few examples below.

School Assemblies. Many agendas for school assemblies consist of 80 percent adults talking and 20 percent student participation. Once an assembly is turned into a leadership event, those percentages are flipped. The assembly may even become entirely student-led.

What makes a leadership-based assembly different from a typical assembly is when the students planning the assembly put on their leadership glasses and view the agenda from a leadership perspective by asking such questions as: "What is the purpose of the assembly?" "Is it more than entertainment?" "How do we use the assembly to build community and trust?" "How will we strengthen students' self-confidence and acceptance of others as a result of the assembly?" "Whose talents can we showcase?" "Whose contributions can we acknowledge by making deposits in their Emotional Bank Accounts?"

Principal Dr. Kim Cummins knows well the value of using assemblies to unite her students. Every Friday morning for twenty minutes, all students and staff gather to enjoy what they call Synergy Assemblies. It was her teachers' idea. Initially, Dr. Cummins was nervous that doing it every week might take away from learning time. Yet for years now, every Friday morning the whole school has met first thing to talk about how they are progressing toward their school goals and to celebrate positive things that happened during the week. Students run the entire assembly. It is obvious by the volume of students' cheers that they love the weekly celebrations.

At secondary schools, no assembly should pass by without the amazing talents of students being displayed and recognized. On occasion, students may vote to bring in a guest speaker or have one of their teachers conduct a portion of the assembly. Students are excellent at finding ways to celebrate their teachers' talents. We attended one assembly when the students invited one of their teachers to open it by playing a song on his electric guitar. He had the place rocking! But assembly is ultimately a matter of students gathering to celebrate each other's voices.

In fact, some *Leader in Me* schools have expanded the number of school assemblies by adding a handful of talent showcases. They are opportunities for peers to celebrate peers. Not all are full assemblies but, rather, smaller orchestrated opportunities for short performances to highlight talents and progress. For example, several schools set aside days to celebrate artwork that students have created in their art classes. Some have choir or orchestra performances for their peers. Some have drama clubs that perform short plays. One school had a Chinese Yo-Yo Club perform. Several have dance teams perform. A.B. Combs has a ball-bouncing event where students bounce balls in rhythm, and it is impressive. Some provide lunchtime entertainment. All are student-planned and student-led.

Leadership Days. An event that A.B. Combs started and turned into a tradition is Leadership Day. It started out of necessity. The school was getting so many calls from educators wanting to experience the school that it was turning into something of a burden. They decided to consolidate visitors by having them come on designated days, twice a year. On each occasion, over one hundred guests arrive and spend the day hearing from teachers, students, and parents about their best practices and *Leader in Me* celebrations. Students share their talents and academic progress. Teachers host guests in their classrooms and showcase their creative resources and strategies. An entire day could be spent exploring the physical environment.

More than anything, however, the day is an event for students to practice and display their leadership skills. Students do most of the speaking parts. Some dance, sing, have art displayed, do skits, oversee booths, play musical instruments, act as greeters, serve food, manage the audio/visual equipment, lead tours, and share other talents. Students help with planning, creating invitations, and writing thank-you notes. They come away feeling more confident about themselves and their leadership skills. It gives all students and teachers a chance to tell part of their story.

The Leadership Day tradition has since spread to hundreds of schools. Virtually every school across the globe in more than fifty countries will hold a Leadership Day once a year. As you might expect, they are all different. No two are alike. They make it their own.

One elementary school student was eager to participate in Leadership Day, but he didn't think he had a talent to share. With some thinking, he realized that he came from a family of hunters. He had learned how to make duck calls, so that is what he shared as a talent on Leadership Day.

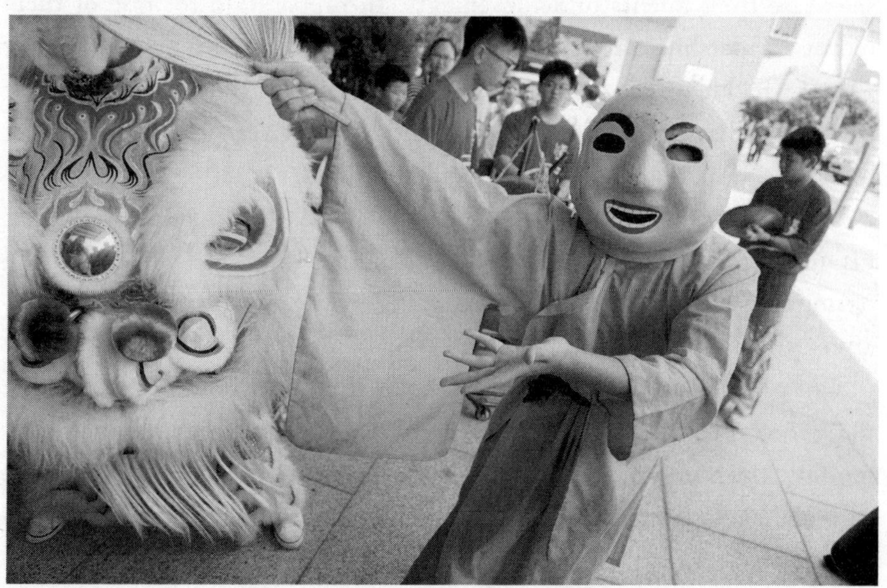

Students showcase students' cultural traditions as a way
of expanding leadership understanding.

No ducks showed up, but he did get a few quacks and roaring applause from the audience. He was proud of himself. Every child deserves an audience.

Some schools are so distant from other locations that it can be challenging to find guests to attend. So they get creative. One school was in an outlying farming community and unable to attract a lot of guests, so they chose to get the community involved. Local farmers brought in their latest and fanciest tractors and some farm animals for all the students to experience. The farmers shared leadership insights with the students, and, in turn, the students and teachers shared leadership talents and school with the farmers. Many parents attended, which provided an excellent audience for the students and teachers. They did it their way.

North Henderson High School calls their Leadership Day a Leadership Showcase. It lasts for three hours, and students plan and lead the whole thing. Tours are given. Students share their leadership portfolios (to be described later) to visitors. Community guests participate. A student panel talks about their personal leadership journeys. Students apply to showcase their talents or achievements. In preparation for one of their recent Leadership Showcases, one of the quietest students applied to participate. He was a student who always wore black leather jackets, black pants, and black boots, and scarcely said a word. Yet when it came time for Leadership Day, he said, "I play guitar, and I want to use my talent as a way of welcoming guests when they arrive." More impressive than his guitar playing was how he blossomed after that. He referred to the opportunity as his "coming-out party," because he was much more social after that.

One principal refers to Leadership Day as "the Super Bowl of the year" for the school. A teacher said, "We invite everybody who is important in the community, which means everybody. It's a day for us to showcase how awesome we are and how *Leader in Me* has changed us all. It's a huge deal here. It really, really is."

Morning Announcements. A common event at many non–*Leader in Me* schools is morning announcements. What *Leader in Me* schools do a

Students sing why they are "Wild About Leadership" for guests at a Leadership Day event.

little differently is to turn them into leadership events by handing responsibility for leading the morning announcements over to students. It is a schoolwide opportunity for students to practice their public speaking skills while making everyone aware of important or interesting events or information. Students do the planning, interview guests, and announce any special news or events.

For schools that have multimedia talent and technology, students like to create videos that consist of interviewing guests or welcoming new people to the school. Or they create videos that highlight various leadership principles. They telecast their work for all students to see. Students typically love student-created videos, especially when their peers are highlighted in positive, fun ways.

Alumni Events. A fun tradition in some districts and schools is to invite graduating high school seniors back to their elementary schools to celebrate and remember their years in the district. At Pauline-Glenn Springs Elementary, for example, all graduating high school seniors return to the school dressed in their graduation cap and gown, and are greeted by the elementary school students who line the hallways to see them. The students give the seniors a high five, and then they all go out and play a game of kickball.

Similarly, at Northwest School District, a *Leader in Me* district in Missouri, all graduating seniors return to their elementary school for a celebration dinner. Again, it is a way of celebrating their full preK–12 years of being a part of the district. About that same time of year, the district's high school honors three or four alumni and has them speak to the students prior to being inducted into the Alumni Hall of Fame.

Class Meetings. Some of the more important and impactful events in a school are not the big schoolwide events but, rather, the simple, daily events that happen in the classroom.

Most *Leader in Me* classrooms in elementary schools hold consistent times each day when they get together to discuss how well the class is doing, plan classroom events, remind everyone of classroom expectations, or do something fun to celebrate a class success. Or they use the time to talk about events of the week or read a funny book. It is time to build connections. Some refer to these times as class meetings or "circle time." It is a time to teach the *7 Habits* or other leadership principles. Instead of the teacher doing all the leading, students take turns leading discussions, planning projects, creating class expectations, or practicing public speaking.

Secondary schools may have advisory periods, academies, houses, or homeroom classes, and they are used for the same purposes, such as learning leadership principles or students connecting with each other. They ensure that every secondary student has at least one teacher with a specific assignment to look out for their well-being.

Many elementary school teachers find it valuable to bookend classroom meetings at the start and finish of each day as a way of setting goals and then talking about how things went that day, what goals they achieved, and so forth. Such moments are great opportunities for teachers to model the *7 Habits* and use them as a framework for listening and problem-solving.

Share Leadership

You might recall that two of the five core paradigms of *Leader in Me* are "Everyone can be a leader" and "Everyone has genius." Nowhere is this more visible than when everyone is given responsibilities to be leaders.

Indeed, a significant portion of what students see, hear, and feel every day at *Leader in Me* schools is everyone being leaders and discovering and utilizing their voice. That includes all students, all teachers and administrators, all office team members, cafeteria crew, counselors, librarians, aides, technology experts, custodians, bus drivers, safety officers, volunteers, nurses, playground supervisors, and so forth—everyone.

At one *Leader in Me* school, the custodian was asked to greet students as they arrived at the morning carpool location. He was there every morning welcoming students, calling them by name, saying encouraging things, and bringing cheer to start the day. He did the same in the hallways throughout his day. All the students liked him. He was a leader. That is because for this custodian, he saw leadership as a passion, not a position.

The same is true for students who are given meaningful responsibilities. They, too, see their responsibilities as more than mere jobs or chores. They are not told exactly what to do or how to do it. Rather, they are shown the need that must be met, are given the responsibility for figuring out how to best meet that need, and are empowered to carry it out, either alone or with a team. They are leaders.

Research Says . . .

A six-year study jointly carried out by the University of Minnesota and the University of Toronto revealed:

- When leadership is shared among the principal, teachers, staff, students, and parents (collective leadership), it has a stronger influ-

> ence on student achievement than when the principal is seen as sole leader.
>
> - Principals do not lose influence as others gain influence.
> - School leaders impact student achievement more by improving teachers' motivation and working conditions than they do by attempting to increase teachers' knowledge and skills.
> - High-performing schools award greater decision-making influence to teacher teams, parents, and, in particular, students than do low-performing schools.

Three specific ways that students are given leadership responsibilities are: being part of a lighthouse or action team, being responsible for a leadership role at the school or classroom level, and being asked to share their insights and voices.

Lighthouse and Action Teams

Lighthouse teams consist of adults and students who are heavily involved in improving the school's physical environment, setting the tone of the social-emotional environment, and planning and carrying out leadership events. They are referred to as "lighthouse" members because they provide direction and act as role models.

When a school first launches *Leader in Me*, an adult lighthouse team is formed and empowered to decide how best to launch. Team members are selected because of their various talents and respected influence with adults and students. They may include the principal, other administrators, a school counselor, a few teachers from multiple grade levels or departments, and perhaps a parent or two. A main responsibility of the group is to select the student lighthouse team.

The student lighthouse team is also formed and empowered early in the process. In most cases, the students of the lighthouse team become the face of

Leader in Me for students. They plan and lead assemblies, provide feedback to administrators, and lead student action teams. In many schools, students apply to be on the lighthouse team, but adults are always careful to ensure that the team is representative of all students, not just the students who are usually selected to be leaders.

The student lighthouse team is often kept to twelve to twenty students, though some high schools include many more students. In fact, we have seen teams of eighty or more because so many students want to participate. However, in such cases, it is wise to keep the main lighthouse team small and to create action teams to share the leadership responsibilities for planning and leading events or projects.

Being on the lighthouse team is life-changing for some students. One high school principal told us about a young woman who, in her freshman year, was considered an "at risk" student. More than her attendance, teachers worried about her emotional well-being. She had hinted at self-harm. Yet in talking with her one day, the principal thought to invite her to join the lighthouse team. To his surprise, she readily accepted. She had never been trusted like

A student lighthouse team discusses plans for an upcoming leadership event.

that before. By her senior year, she was leading the student lighthouse team, confidently speaking in front of hundreds of adults, and happily heading to a university—the first in her family to do so.

At North Henderson High School, students are given the opportunity to suggest action teams to focus on what they see as being important needs or causes. It gives them a sense of purpose and connectedness. For example, there is a landscape club that is in charge of beautifying the campus's exterior grounds. There is an interior beautification club that takes responsibility for the interior appearance of the building. There is a "Planet Purple" club that has responsibility for recycling and composting. There is a "Good News" club that features students' and teachers' accomplishments and interests. There is a spirit team that hypes up school spirit on days when there is a sports event happening. In all, the principal told us that the school went from having about thirty students to nearly five hundred students participating in "leadership" roles.

When Principal Dr. Jill Scheulen's middle school was first getting underway with *Leader in Me*, she and her staff began looking for authentic opportunities for students to take on leadership roles. They could come up with only a handful of ideas, and yet there were nearly a thousand students. So they decided to ask the students for ideas. The students exploded with all kinds of ideas. A few students suggested collecting used sporting equipment for needy children in the school's area. They sent out a notice for volunteers to help. Seventy-five volunteered, far more than they needed. So they divided tasks and formed a marketing team, a sorting team, a celebration team, and so forth. It was all run by students during noninstructional times. It was a great service learning opportunity—all student-led.

In some cases, the lighthouse team takes the form of a for-credit class. They meet daily, learn leadership skills, and lead several action teams. When trusted, they can have a tremendous impact on the culture of a school.

Leadership Roles

Not all leadership roles involve being on a lighthouse team or action team. Many are temporary assignments and are experienced at either the school or

Students plan, present, and handle the technology for
the morning news from start to finish.

classroom level. Many leadership roles originate with the adults asking, "What
can students do that adults are currently doing?"

What follows is an example of students filling a leadership role at the elementary school level, followed by a few examples at the secondary school
level. Consider what a powerful impact the opportunity to lead can have on
students, starting with Olivia.

When we first met Olivia, she was a third-grade student in New York. She
was an above-average student academically, and she was also a selective mute.
She spoke freely at home, but from the onset of kindergarten she had chosen
not to say a word at school. The only word any teacher had heard from her was
a one-sentence recording she had made at home for her third-grade teacher,
Mrs. Talty. It was part of a holiday gift.

So imagine the surprise on Mrs. Talty's face on the day Olivia raised her
hand to volunteer to speak about one of the habits at the school's Leader-

ship Day. It meant speaking in front of two hundred adults. As ecstatic as Mrs. Talty was, she had every reason to fear that Olivia might panic when the time came for her to do her part. Yet Mrs. Talty also did not want to miss the opportunity to have Olivia share her voice. "Olivia, are you sure?" she asked. And all she got in return was a nod.

Principal Kathy Brachmann was also surprised by Olivia's desire to take on a speaking part on Leadership Day. And she, too, was concerned about placing Olivia in a detrimental situation. So she insisted that Olivia first be given a trial situation. She attempted to talk with Olivia about it for four days in a row, yet each time Olivia held her silence. Finally, on day five, a Friday, Mrs. Brachmann said, "Olivia, I know you want to speak at Leadership Day. If you will recite the Pledge of Allegiance over the speaker system on Monday, you can speak at Leadership Day. Will you do that?" Once again, Olivia's only response was a tentative nod.

Mrs. Brachmann was thrilled Monday morning when she returned to the school after attending a district meeting. She found her staff all smiling through their tears. They told her how Olivia had confidently taken the microphone and, in the sweetest voice, said: "Good morning, I'm Olivia," and then proceeded to recite the pledge without any hesitation. The entire school cheered with joy. But then Olivia went back to her silence.

Eight students were selected to be Leadership Day speakers. Each would be assigned to describe one habit. Mrs. Brachmann asked if any of them had a favorite habit they wanted to speak about. Instantly, up went Olivia's hand. Another big surprise! When asked to identify her habit, out from Olivia's lips trickled a soft reply: "Habit 8: Find Your Voice." The choice alone caught Mrs. Brachmann off guard. She had to hold back tears because of the irony of the habit Olivia had chosen.

Olivia went to work. She researched the 8th Habit. With a little help from her mother, she drafted an outline of what she would say. When Leadership Day finally arrived, everyone wondered, "Will she really do it?" Then, on cue, Olivia stood at the front of the auditorium before the vast audience of adults. Gazing out at all the eyes fixed on her, she hesitated just long enough to put

Mrs. Brachmann and Mrs. Talty on edge. "Come on, Olivia. We know you can do it!" they kept silently pleading.

Then, very calmly, as if the entire day had been made just for her, Olivia began to speak:

> Hi, my name is Olivia from Mrs. Talty's third-grade class. Habit 8 is Find Your Voice, Then Help Others to Find Theirs. . . . To find your voice, you need to examine your natural talent. Everyone is good at something! Don't let anyone convince you otherwise. You can inspire others to do great things. Thank you.

Olivia's mother wept openly. She was so pleased that Olivia was in a school and learning environment where she was loved, respected, and given a chance to contribute. A place where she could literally find her voice.

Now for a few middle school examples.

As the school librarian sat in the *Leader in Me* workshop, she listened to all the teachers discuss what leadership roles they could give to their students. As a librarian, she wondered, "What leadership roles might I give to students? Would any students even offer to help me in the library?"

Days went by, and on her way to the library each morning, she would pass a number of students who were sitting on the floor in the hallway, all by themselves, waiting for the morning bell to ring. Their school bus would drop them off a full thirty minutes before class, and they had nothing to do but wait. While other students mingled with friends, these students appeared to be friendless.

The librarian decided to ask a few of the students to help her sort and shelve books. That went well, so she began asking more hallway students if they would like to volunteer. A few more joined. Each was assigned a section of shelves to straighten, organize, and dust. It didn't require much effort, so they finished quickly and ended up sitting at the library tables laughing and socializing until the first bell rang. By the end of the first semester, the librarian had thirty volunteers. In fact, there were getting to be so many volunteers that she had to assign them to alternating days. Some began checking books out and in and doing other office assignments. It got to the point where about all the librarian needed to do each morning was unlock the door and let the students take over. The students felt valued for their efforts, but mostly they enjoyed the social aspects of the assignment. Not only did it reduce the librarian's workload, but she was also named Teacher of the Year for the school and then the district.

Of course, most leadership responsibilities offered to students are small and not likely to lead to major life-altering outcomes. But there is a good chance they will lead to increased self-worth, self-confidence, self-efficacy, and self-awareness. And those are no small matters. Take Jared's case as an example.

Jared had been sent to his middle school principal's office on multiple occasions, and not for outstanding behavior. His caring parents were distraught and didn't know what to do.

One day, the principal sent for Jared. When Jared arrived at his office, he was wearing a defensive, rebellious, "What did I do?" look on his face. The principal assured Jared that he had done nothing wrong. "I was thinking about you this morning and wondering how things were going," he said. The principal had always been straight with him before, so Jared relaxed. He sensed the principal's sincere interest in him. And, for whatever reason, he opened up about his feelings that day, more than ever before. The principal did very little talking.

A few days later, Jared was again called to the office. During their prior visit, the principal had noticed how articulate Jared was. It had been suggested that students should lead the morning announcements instead of the principal or another adult doing it, and Jared's name had come to his mind.

Jared's eyes lit up when he was offered the role of doing the announcements, even though the agreement was for "One day only!" When students figured out it was Jared making the announcements, they were all surprised. "How come he got to do it?" they wondered.

Jared's "one day" turned into two weeks of doing the announcements. He took the role seriously. However, by the end of the two weeks, the principal was so tired of hearing, "Why does Jared always get to do it?" that he decided to ask Jared if he would take responsibility for leading a student action team for morning announcements. Again, Jared's eyes lit up.

Ultimately, twenty students became part of the action team, with each being assigned in pairs to take turns making morning and afternoon announcements. Jared organized a rotating schedule and thrived in coaching the other students on how to do it. This went on for the rest of the year. It is an enormous understatement to say that Jared's parents were delighted to see him go from wanting nothing to do with school to doing well in school and actively researching potential universities to attend.

These are just three examples of how students can be given opportunities to be leaders and find their voice at a schoolwide level. Other examples of school-level leadership opportunities include leading school tours, being responsible for raising the flag, planning and leading assemblies, leading playground activities, helping in the cafeteria, doing safety patrol, being morning

A student artfully welcomes students to the science
wing of Swain County High School.

greeters, speaking at Leadership Day, teaching lessons, leading clubs, making presentations, and so forth. These same roles can be applied at elementary and secondary school levels, though students might carry them out in entirely different ways depending on their maturity and skill level. Again, most of these roles originate from adults asking, "What am I currently doing that a student could do?"

As students mature, so do their leadership responsibilities. With time they may be teaching lessons, leading projects, mentoring younger students, answering phones, or choosing books for the class to read. Several schools challenge students to organize service projects that benefit the school or community. With teachers or parents as "guides on the side," students identify, plan, and carry out all aspects of the projects.

Now, some people might think, "Those are not all leadership roles, those are jobs." What turns tasks or routine assignments into leadership roles is when the adults turn the responsibility over to students and empower them to perform the responsibility in the way they see fit. They don't micromanage them.

When given the chance, students will come up with many of the best ideas for leadership responsibilities. For example, an elementary school student named Bryson approached Principal Keli Sare and said, "I want to schedule a meeting with you." She responded, "Would you like to talk with me now?" "No, I need more time," he indicated.

So a date was scheduled for a later time. Bryson arrived at the meeting with a multi-slide presentation. He described how he had noticed that many adults end up running their own business, and he thought students should be taught entrepreneurship and business skills so they could be prepared when their time came. His proposal was to host a small business fair. He would put together a small committee and they would meet bimonthly. He proposed a system to allow students to take out small business loans. He wanted students to teach students how to give a proper handshake, along with plenty more ideas. He had it all planned out.

With Ms. Sare's approval, Bryson and his team went to work. The community was invited, and the event was hosted at a small park. Over one hundred parents, community members, and the school superintendent attended. Eight booths were set up with various items prepared for sale by the young entrepreneurs. Every student's booth sold out. One student's booth was for healthy salads. She was contracted by a construction crew to serve them her salads at a later lunch date. Students gave a portion of their earnings back to school to generate more small loans for the next fair. Ms. Sare could only sit back and smile at Bryson and his initiative.

Leadership roles can be a great learning laboratory. At Janson Elementary, each classroom designates a student technology leader. If the teacher ever has a need or problem with any type of technology, that student either sets up the equipment or fixes a problem. If the student cannot fix the problem, then they go to the school's adult technology advisor. The advisor then either teaches the student how to solve the problem, or goes with the student to the classroom and they solve the problem together. The student learns new knowledge and feels the responsibility, while the teacher keeps on teaching.

So how are leadership roles assigned? In some cases, it is a matter of which student needs the opportunity most. In other cases, it is a matter of which student is most capable for the role. In any case, it is a grand learning opportunity for students to go through the process of applying for a leadership role. For instance, media center specialists Mrs. Headly and Ms. Ray post positions for students to help in the media center as assistant librarians, and about fifty students apply at the start of each year. The students fill out applications, obtain a recommendation from a parent and teacher (to ensure that adults know what is going on), and then they get interviewed. Don't tell the students, but all of them get hired. All also learn from experiencing the hiring process and from learning new skills.

It should not be underestimated what impact leadership roles can have on students and their well-being. We can share many stories similar to Jason's. Let's just say that he saw his leadership role in the school as being the local bully. He had just been in a fight with another boy, and his principal and parents didn't know what to do. Suspending him was going to be a reward, not a punishment. But then the principal decided to ask him if he would like to be a member of the flag-raising crew. Each morning, he would need to be on time to help raise the flags in front of the school. There was a process to it, and he would need to learn the process. It was an important role, and Jason liked the idea. He liked it so much that he was chosen the next year to be the flag-raising team leader. He was particular about how the team would do their work, and he was dutiful in letting each team member know how important the role was. He was proud of his role. He was no longer a bully. He was a leader.

Many leadership roles are experienced at the classroom level. Once again, teachers start the process by asking, "What can students do that I typically do?"

Elementary school teachers typically have their students most of the day, so there are a bunch of ways their students can serve or lead out, from being line leaders to pencil sharpener leaders, to leaders of feeding the pets, leaders of passing out assignments, morning greeters, leaders of straightening chairs, bookshelf leaders, music leaders, leaders of humor, videography leaders, and so forth. One elementary school student proudly informed us that he was the class's leader of electricity. He turned the lights on and off and was proud of it.

Middle school math teacher Stephanie Miller was trying to think of roles her students could take on in her classroom. She came up with a few but decided to ask her class: "What am I doing that you could be doing?" She was surprised by their responses. Her daily routine was to start class by having students solve a math problem as a warm-up activity. Afterward, she would lead a discussion of who got it right, what worked, what were common mistakes, and so forth. The students said, "We can lead that discussion." So Ms. Miller gave them the stage. She created a sign-up sheet for students to volunteer for a day, and in no time the sheet was completely filled. Other students handed out and collected assignments at the start of class. The students came up with the idea that the students who led the day's math challenge should get to sit at a special parlor table in the back of the room. They thought it was fun. She didn't tell them that the previous year that table was specifically reserved for students with disruptive discipline issues.

Mentoring is one of the more popular leadership roles students like to take on. Older students mentor younger students in academic assignments or in modeling proper behavior. An entire class of upper-grade student leaders might be assigned to mentor a younger class of students. At Northeast High School in Macon, Georgia, some star athletes in the school took it upon themselves to mentor younger students. In some cases, they chose to mentor students who they worried might be at risk for dropping out of school. The mentored students were thrilled to have a star athlete take an interest in them and be a friend. What made it special for the mentored students was that they knew their star mentors were doing it by choice. It wasn't just a job they were assigned to do.

Andre Deshotel, a behavior coach at Martin Petitjean Elementary, mentions that for students dealing with anxiety, the right roles can relieve some of their stress as they focus on their leadership roles rather than their anxieties. A principal in Florida agrees, using her elementary school–age son as an example.

The Student Lighthouse Team at East High School plans and sets goals, as their advisor guides from the side.

Her son suffered from anxiety when he was a student at her school. But he was also fascinated by his teacher's microphone. His teacher noticed. She assigned him the leadership role of using the microphone to welcome his peers to class each day. That was all he needed to do for his leadership role—take the microphone and welcome his peers to class.

The next year, his new teacher (at the advice of his previous teacher) raised him up a level by asking him to use the microphone to lead some of the morning announcements. He did it throughout the year. By the time the principal's son was ready to leave elementary school, he was confident to the point that he was assigned to be the emcee for the school's Leadership Day, with nearly a hundred adults in attendance. Today, he is graduating from high school with a Top 10 recognition and an associate of arts degree from a local college.

One mother noted, "My daughter gets very excited about school because she has a role where she can lead others. It gives her confidence. She struggles a bit with schoolwork, so for her to be able to have something apart from academics that she can be proud of has been really positive for her. She'll say, 'Mom, I need to be at the school on this night. I'm going to help be in charge of this program we are doing.' She has lots of opportunities to shine in non-academic ways that she did not have at her previous schools."

Many teachers like to create charts to track various leadership roles. They also like to rotate assignments every few weeks so students have opportunities to try new assignments and enjoy variation. When assignments are changed and students see on the chart that they have a new role, they simply go to work. Not a lot of explanation is needed.

One visitor to a middle school saw a leadership role chart in a classroom and asked the teacher—who was between classes—how it worked. Instead of explaining how it worked, she said, "Just stay here and watch." As students arrived, one started collecting homework, one started passing out the previous day's homework, another cleared the whiteboard from the previous class, another recognized the birthdays of the week, and so forth. The teacher never said a word. The students arrived and took over. They felt ownership. They felt appreciated.

The important thing to point out is that, in each of the previously discussed situations, the thing that changed first was the educator's paradigm of their role and the paradigm they had of the students. Instead of viewing each student as someone who needed to be controlled or managed, they saw students as individuals who needed to be led. They saw students' worth and potential and worked from the paradigm of "Leadership is communicating a person's worth and potential so clearly that they are inspired to see it in themselves."

Like everything with *Leader in Me*, leadership roles are meant for everyone. Literally everyone. In a school of eight hundred students, with a little work and creativity, every student can have a meaningful leadership role that is aligned to what they're good at and what they love to do. Leadership is not just for the same ten students who seem to get asked every year to take on a leadership role. One visitor had tears in his eyes when he told us about walking into a special education classroom. One of the students came toward him, took him by the hand, and led him to where he needed to go. She was being a leader even though she was nonverbal. She brought him to her desk and started sharing her work with him. Nobody prompted her.

Many teachers are often surprised at how well students can lead projects, and come away thinking, "Why didn't we do this earlier?" We were working with one set of middle school teachers, and when we spoke to them about students taking over leadership roles—roles that the adults would typically do—they thought it was crazy. They couldn't imagine students doing those roles. A year later, they couldn't imagine why it took them so many years to figure out that it is actually a better way of doing things, and that in many cases it makes their roles as teachers easier and more rewarding. As students grow in maturity, so too do the opportunities for leadership roles: Secondary schools often include roles like project managers, teacher assistants, substitute leaders, superintendent advisory leaders, Inner Club Council facilitators, and more.

Student Voice

Educators in *Leader in Me* schools don't reactively wait for students to complain or give input about how things are going at the school—they proactively seek out students' voices. They want to know students' ideas for how to make their school and their classrooms more engaging. Even pre-K students have opinions and insights that matter.

How far A.B. Combs is willing to go in seeking students' voices on important matters is evidenced by the fact that before a teaching candidate is offered a position, they get interviewed by a panel of students. And according to new teachers, the student interviewers have a reputation for asking some of the toughest questions. Students have a knack for picking out teachers who like (or do not like) being with students, which is something that is often difficult for adults to detect. One applicant for a teaching position at A.B. Combs was graded low by her student interviewers because, as the students exclaimed with disgust, "She didn't even know we were a *7 Habits* school! She didn't do her homework!"

The spirit of why it is important to listen to student voices is captured in an incident at Heritage Elementary. The school was only three months into implementation of *Leader in Me* when nine principals and an assistant superintendent from the district showed up for a visit to see the "new" model. Students led them on a tour. At the conclusion, the group gathered in the foyer to ask questions. The principal had the students do the responding. One visitor asked, "What is different in your school now that you are doing *Leader in Me*?" A fifth-grade student named Grant stepped forward. Using his hands to motion, he said, "It used to be [that] the principal was up here (raising his hand above his head), and the teachers were here (putting his hand chin high), and the students were down here (holding his hand belly button high). Now," he continued, "it feels like the principal, the teachers, and the students are all at the same level (sliding his hand horizontally all at chin height). We are all working together."

A student from Sweden put it this way, "It used to be that the only time we went to the office was when we were sent to the office for misbehavior. Now, anytime we think something needs to be changed, we go to the principal's office with our suggestion."

The same measure of respect is given to students in classrooms. As noted previously, many classrooms hold class meetings to seek student opinions on how to improve daily routines or classroom behaviors. Several teachers establish suggestion boxes or assign student advocates (another option for a leadership role) who voice student opinions. Students' best help is not in identifying problems but in identifying solutions. It is not just a gimmick to make students feel good. Student opinions are earnestly sought after and sincerely valued.

Some elementary school classrooms hold circle time. They sit on the carpet in a circle. They supply and review any feedback that they or their teacher feel is important. Teachers find it a useful way to discuss issues regarding data on discipline matters, attendance, and achievement, or to discuss if there are things they as a teacher can improve, or to find out what is happening on the playground.

Such times are more typical for elementary school classrooms, but the same principle applies to secondary school classrooms. On occasion, teachers may pause and ask, "How are things going as a class?" "How can I make things easier to understand?" One teacher did that, and the students all erupted at the same time, "You scheduled a big exam for this Friday. It's the day of prom,

A panel of high school students demonstrate leadership, confidence, and communication skills in responding to questions.

the big dance. What were you thinking?" The teacher had never even thought of the conflict with prom. He shifted the date to the loud cheers of students. They felt their voices were being heard.

Some classes use quality tools or graphic organizers to collect feedback. For example, a plus/delta chart. Pluses are what is going well, and deltas are suggestions for improvement. Students can put items on both sides of the chart and then the class can discuss them. Some teachers like to use other graphic organizers such as bubble maps, affinity diagrams, or force-field analysis. Entire books have been written about how to use these tools to get students talking. Suffice it to say that students enjoy using the tools to

Students learn to focus on what they can control as
a way of leading from the inside-out.

problem-solve, brainstorm ideas, analyze stories, plan projects, set goals, and establish class rules.

A tool that *Leader in Me* schools can optimize is the Measurable Results Assessment (MRA). It sends out a survey and collects feedback from teachers, staff, students, and parents, and aggregates a report. When Natcher Elementary first launched *Leader in Me*, Principal Matt Thornhill was intrigued but a bit skeptical about the thought of collecting survey data from students. "What kind of feedback might our students offer?" he wondered. But once students had submitted their feelings about how they felt things were going at the school, Mr. Thornhill found their insights tremendously helpful. He says, "We do a lot of surveys now. Both with the adults and with our students. Students feel like they have a voice in the school. And we have truly come to see the value in synergy and getting more people's ideas involved. It has helped me as a leader to not try to lead from the top down."

Once educators catch the spirit of students sharing their voice, they don't want to return to not asking students for their voice on important matters. Of course, there will be times when administrators or teachers must say no to student requests or insights. Giving students voice does not mean that adults give students everything they want. But it does mean making the effort and time for students and adults to seek to understand each other.

In Summary

"Given the challenges we face," declared Sir Ken Robinson, "education doesn't need to be reformed—it needs to be transformed. The key to this transformation is not to standardize education, but to personalize it, to build achievement on discovering the individual talents of each child, to put students in an environment where they want to learn and where they can naturally discover their true passions."[1] Isn't that exactly what this chapter has been about? Providing a stimulating, nurturing learning environment for students.

Students want to learn in that type of school and classroom culture, a culture where they feel good about themselves and are offered opportunities to contribute and blossom. And it is important to remember that teachers and other adults in a school also want to work and thrive within a positive school culture. They, too, want to feel valued. They, too, have much to contribute. Across the world, we have seen many office personnel, custodians, cafeteria workers, and volunteers blossom by being involved in participating in each of the components of a leadership culture. In many cases, their lives have been changed. So, don't forget! *Leader in Me* is designed as much for the adults as it is for the students.

But none of it happens, for either students or teachers, without intentional effort and built-in systems to support the culture. A school's culture requires proactive attention and consistent nurturing, and cannot be left to chance.

Our experience is that a school's culture starts with the adults in the school.

Secondary schools may have several small student-led action teams to plan and lead specific leadership events.

When the adults in the school truly believe in students, students come to believe in themselves. In our research with *Teacher Believed in Me*, we have learned that students will feel the adults believe in them when they feel the adults:

1. Accept students as they are; help them feel *connection*.
2. Teach them about life; bring *meaning* to why they go to school.
3. Inspire them to see their strengths; give them a sense of *hope*.
4. Entrust them with responsibility; allow them to experience their *self-worth*.
5. Help them through a hard time; build their *resilience*.
6. Empower them to help themselves; strengthen their *self-efficacy*.
7. Correct them in positive ways; enable them to see their *growth*.[2]

When the adults possess those leadership skillsets and integrate them into the culture of a school, students will come to believe in themselves. Students will become more ready to learn.

5

Aligning for Academic Results

A parent of an elementary school student shared the following recollection of how she was introduced to *Leader in Me*:

I'm a working mom. Two years ago I attended an executive development program with leaders from highly successful companies. It focused on getting back to the basics. What were those basics?

- Working on our company cultures
- Setting goals for our companies
- Setting goals for ourselves
- Encouraging collaboration
- Tracking progress
- Analyzing our failures
- Celebrating successes

A few months later, I was at our elementary school when the principal announced they would be embracing *Leader in Me* and the *7 Habits*. I remembered taking the *7 Habits* workshop when I worked for a marketing company. I thought, "How can those habits apply to elementary school students?"

Soon, murals and posters began going up on the school walls. Each class made a mission statement and set class goals. The fact that my son, a fourth grader, could explain how the class mission statement supported the school's mission was amazing to me.

Teachers modeled for students how to achieve personal goals. When teachers fell short on their goals, they talked openly with students about why the goal was not achieved and how they were making adjustments. This was all the same stuff I'd been taught in the executive development program!

Parent-teacher conferences were entirely student-led. I'd never experienced anything like it. My son was excited to show me his leadership portfolio that contained his goals and successes. He used it to discuss his academic progress. He knew exactly which tests he had done poorly on and what he needed to do to improve. I was blown away.

What this parent could have added is that in just two years her son's school went from 36 percent of students passing the state reading exams to 67 percent passing.

The 4 Disciplines of Execution

Leader in Me is not an academic program per se. It does not teach math strategies or how to read and write. It does not offer science, history, or technology curricula. What *Leader in Me* does do is provide leadership principles and tools that enable district leaders, teachers, and students to align for academic results.

What does it mean to align for academic results?

This chapter answers that question. It introduces a new set of leadership skills that are embedded in a process known as *The 4 Disciplines of Execution for Educators*. (The process is described in detail in a companion book with the same name.[1]) The first half of this chapter describes each of the *4 Disciplines* and provides examples of how to apply them as an individual, a class or team, and a school. The second half of the chapter then recommends three leadership tools that teachers can use to empower students to take ownership of their learning.

Most educators are effective at *setting* goals. They do it often. What they readily admit, however, is that they are less effective at *achieving* goals. In other words, too often goals are set at the beginning of the year and then tucked away in an orderly drawer, where they are left unbothered for some time.

The *4 Disciplines* is a tested process for both setting and achieving goals. They are used by top leaders and top companies around the world to produce better personal and organizational results. Each requires discipline.

There are at least three general types of goals:

Checklist Goals: "I have a goal to go to bed on time tonight." Or "I have a goal to have my homework done before seven o'clock tonight." Such goals are short-term and can be checked off as soon as completed. Check. Done. Finished. Signed off with the stroke of a pen.

Project-Based Goals: "We have a goal to improve family engagement at our school, and there are five components of the project." Or "I have a goal to redo all the bulletin boards in my classroom a week before school starts." Such goals can be short-term or long-term, and have multiple parts—a task list of items—for completion.

Behavior-Change Goals. "I have a goal to lose fifteen pounds by the end of the school year." Or "I have a goal to improve my reading scores by ten percent by the end of the semester." These goals tend to be longer-term. They require a change of behavior or an increase in skill level to achieve them. They require extra discipline.

The *4 Disciplines* are designed for and focused specifically on achieving behavior-change goals that require a person or team to change behaviors, such as breaking an old habit or gaining a new habit, improving reading skills, increasing attendance, and so forth. The *4 Disciplines* are: 1. Focus on the Wildly Important; 2. Act on the Lead Measures; 3. Keep a Compelling Scoreboard, and 4. Create a Cadence of Accountability. Brief descriptions of each follow.

Discipline 1: Focus on the Wildly Important

Most goals that people set are important. But only a few goals are "Wildly Important Goals." We fondly refer to them as WIGs. A WIG is a goal that really matters, a goal that is so important that no other success can compensate for failure to achieve this goal.

To appreciate what a WIG is, think of all that teachers do in a day or week as being part of their "whirlwind." Lesson planning. Grading assignments. Crafting exams. Contacting parents. Managing classroom behaviors. Meeting required learning standards. Taking attendance. Listening to excuses. Coaching a sports team. Mentoring a club. Writing reports. Meeting with a grade-level team. Preparing a daily agenda. Gathering supplies. Resolving conflicts. Organizing shelves. Making copies. And on and on goes the list. It can feel like a whirlwind.

Administrators also have their own whirlwind or sets of whirlwinds. In fact, it has been said that they have over one hundred roles. And when their personal and family whirlwinds get added to their professional whirlwinds, things can start spinning around at faster and faster speeds. If you are an administrator, you know the feeling.

Students experience their own whirlwinds. We recently interviewed a group of middle school students, all of whom were outstanding students. We asked them to identify their biggest challenge as teens. We expected answers like peer pressure, loneliness, family troubles, and such. Their first answers all dealt with not being able to balance and prioritize everything they were supposed to do in life. Between class assignments, after-school activities, time with friends, and demands from parents, they simply did not know how to deal with it all. Their eyeballs were practically spinning like whirlwinds as they told us about all the "priorities" adults were putting on them.

So how do teachers, administrators, other school staff, and students survive their whirlwinds? The answer is that they outsmart them. Or at least they bring them down to a manageable size.

When people pause and examine all the "important" tasks their whirlwinds contain, they quickly realize that only a few of the tasks are "Wildly Important." They are the one, two, or three priorities that if not addressed in a timely manner will lead to the greatest pains. In a school setting, they are the specific tasks that if done properly will enable a school to achieve its highest purpose. Schools, classrooms, or individuals will struggle to set or achieve a WIG if they have not first identified their core purpose or mission.

WIGs can often be determined by asking, "What is the one thing that if I (or we) were to do it well would have the greatest impact on my (or our) __________?" For example, what is the one thing that would have the greatest impact on my academics, or my health, or my relationship with my peer teachers if I were to change my (or our) behavior or do it consistently well?

Any remaining goals that are in the whirlwind but are not a WIG are at best a PIG—a Pretty Important Goal. PIGs are also important, but they should not be pursued at the expense of a WIG. After all, if a PIG is not achieved, it may cause only minor pain when compared to the pain that is felt when a WIG is not met. This is why setting no more than one to three WIGs will help a school focus its energies and resources on what matters most.

For a WIG to be most effective and achievable, it must have a clear X (a starting place, where you are now), a clear Y (a destination, the desired outcome), and a clear target for completion (the goal will be reached by when). We call these "X to Y by When goals." For example, a popular personal WIG people choose is to lose weight. In such a case, a person might set a WIG on January 1 that reads: "I will go from 190 pounds to 170 pounds by June 1." When there is not a clear "X to Y by When" target, it is more of an intention or a hope than it is a goal. Good intentions seldom lead to action.

When setting an individual WIG, do not set a goal that is dependent on another person or persons—including students—changing their behaviors. Set goals that are dependent on you changing your behavior. And when setting a team or schoolwide WIG, involve as many of the people who will be pursuing the WIG as is possible. No involvement, no commitment.

People who define their WIGs in a clear, purposeful way are well on their way to slaying the most challenging parts of their whirlwind. As the old saying goes, a goal well-defined is a goal half-achieved.

Discipline 2: Act on the Lead Measures

The second discipline is to "act on the lead measures." To know what that means, it is helpful to know about "lag measures."

Lag measures are what gets measured at the end of a goal period, such as the end of a term or school year. Scores from standardized exams given at the end of a school year are an example of lag measures. They are called lag measures because they come after the work has already happened. There is nothing more that can be done after that point, other than to set a new WIG. For the person setting a WIG to go from 190 pounds to 170 pounds by June 1, the lag measure would be the amount the person weighs on June 1.

In contrast, lead measures are the action steps that must be taken to move the lag measure. In the case of going from 190 to 170 pounds, a lead measure might be to avoid sugar every day and to increase the number of steps taken every day. Lead measures are something you can influence, and they are predictive. If, for example, you eat fewer calories and take more steps, you can predict that you will lose weight. This seems rather obvious, but the fact is lead measures take discipline to track, and that's why they are often ignored. In the case of a sales professional, the lag measure is the total sales amount achieved while the lead measure might be how many face-to-face meetings the salesperson has with customers each week. Organizations of all kinds are full of lag measures and usually lack lead measures. The key is to act on the lead measures, not to wait and see how the lag measures turn out.

At the start of the school year, one kindergarten classroom set a WIG to move from only three kids who could count to one hundred to all twenty-eight kids in the class who could count to one hundred by January 31. They then set two lead measures to help them get there. Lead measure #1 was to count to one hundred every day in class. Lead measure #2 was to practice counting to one hundred at home four times per week. These leads were then tracked and recorded by students. As you can imagine, this class was successful in achieving the WIG. The key, as always, is acting on and tracking the lead measures.

As with the number of WIGs a person or team pursues at any one time, it is strongly suggested that a person commit to acting on no more than one, two, or three action steps or lead measures at a time. It brings focus to the goal-setting process.

Once the key action steps or lead measures are identified, the most important part of Discipline 2 is to have the discipline to consistently act on the lead measures. To not eat that tempting sugar. To get out and exercise. When a person is disciplined in consistently changing their behaviors, they are "acting on the lead measures."

It is important to also track how consistently the person or team is acting on the lead measures. Which brings us to Discipline 3.

Discipline 3: Keep a Compelling Scoreboard

How does a person (or team) know if they are ahead, on pace, or behind in their quest to achieve their WIG? The answer is: Keep a running score.

Imagine a group of students playing a sport. They are casually playing around and having fun. But then what happens as soon as someone starts to keep score? Can you envision their energy levels rise? Do you see their competitive spirits beginning to come out? Can you see how determined they can be to win?

Now imagine a student playing a video game. Watch how engaged the student can get when seeing that his score is rising and rising and approaching an all-time high score. What do you think will happen if the computer crashes and the scoreboard is lost? How long will the student continue playing? Chances are it will not be for long. That is because there is something about buzzers, flashing lights, positive feedback, and exceeding previous scores that seems to magically retain students' (and adults') attention. People play differently when they're keeping score.

Now this time imagine a basketball team playing a game where only the coach knows the score. The players may have a rough sense of whether they are winning or losing, but only the coach knows for sure. And what if that coach tells the players the score only once a quarter? Does that sound ludicrous? Or does it sound familiar? If it sounds familiar, it may be because that is how some teachers operate. Their students work all quarter long without knowing their progress, their scores. Then, at the end of a quarter—or grading period—the teacher finally provides students with their scores. Could that be one reason why some students don't like the game of school?

As with sports and video games, public scoreboards can be powerful tools for achieving WIGs. To be effective, scoreboards must be simple enough that an adult or student can easily glance at them and quickly, within five seconds, tell if they are on track, ahead, or behind in achieving their WIG. They also must be visible for everyone to see, not just the coach. They will track:

* Progress toward the lead measures. For example, show monthly weight loss.
* How disciplined the person is in acting on the lead measures. For example, a calendar marking the days the person ate no sugar and did thirty minutes of exercise.
* A trend line showing where the person should be at various milestones. For example, a line graph showing how much the person should weigh at the start of each month if they are losing two pounds each month.

What student or adult does not like to see that they are progressing? They want to feel that their efforts are helping them achieve their goals. When they can see themselves "winning" against the trend line, it motivates them to keep going. That being said, no public-facing scoreboard should display a student's low scores, weaknesses, or lack of progress in ways that might demotivate or diminish the student's feelings of self-worth.

Discipline 4: Create a Cadence of Accountability

It is said that "goals should be stars to steer by, not sticks with which to beat ourselves." And that is how accountability is intended to be viewed when reviewing progress toward a WIG. It is meant to be a positive, consistent time to review progress. It is an opportunity for students to say, "Hey, look at how well I did!" And it is also a chance for them to reevaluate: "This isn't quite working. I need to adjust the actions I chose."

People are more likely to stick with a goal and achieve it when an accountability partner is involved in the process. An accountability partner (or an "accountabili-buddy," as some students prefer to say it) is aware of the goal, cares about helping the person achieve it, and regularly expresses truthful confidence in the person pursuing the goal: "You are doing great! You can do this!" It is someone who will ask, "How's it going? How can I help?" It is also someone who is willing to challenge: "Are you sure you set the goal high enough?" "Are you being honest with yourself about your progress?" It is someone who provides a friendly second perspective. It is not someone who will scold or condemn.

Consistent check-in times to meet with an accountability partner are called WIG sessions, or "a cadence of accountability." If done consistently, a regular cadence can have tremendous impact on whether a person achieves their WIG. Whether the WIG sessions are held once a week or once a day will depend on the urgency of the WIG and the nature of the person pursuing the WIG. Our

An interactive classroom scoreboard visually tracks Emotional Bank Account deposits and encourages a Win-Win spirit.

recommendation is to hold them weekly, as a week is a perfect unit of time—enough that you can get something done but not so much that you have to wait too long to check in.

Not to be forgotten as an important part of accountability sessions are the celebrations. Celebrations can include high fives, applause, or even small prizes. The biggest celebration, and the one to emphasize most, will be the attainment of a meaningful milestone or the full completion of the WIG. It is the satisfaction of knowing, "I did it." "I can do hard things!" "I completed something meaningful." It is the feeling of having better physical health when the desired weight is achieved in a healthy manner.

So what happens if, at the start of each month, the person weighs himself and is losing only one pound per month? In other words, his lead measures are showing he is one pound short of his goal each month. In that case, the accountability session would be a good time to evaluate whether the goal was too ambitious, whether the key actions (sugar and exercise) were the correct lead measures, or whether the person is not staying disciplined in acting on the lead measures. Again, it is not a time to beat oneself down. Rather it is a time to readjust, recommit, and celebrate any partial progress that has transpired.

Achieve Goals

Wildly Important Goals can be pursued by individuals, teams, and entire schools or districts. The disciplines stay the same, but more communication, cooperation, and synergy are needed as more people are involved with achieving the goal. Without involvement, earnest commitment cannot be expected.

Individual Goals

So with that as a brief overview of the *4 Disciplines*, let's look at what an individual student and teacher setting an academic WIG might look like.

For starters, we point out that even young students are more capable of identifying an academic WIG than many adults give them credit for. Dana

Penick, one of our premier coaches, was teaching a group of elementary school teachers about the *4 Disciplines*, and at one point she asked if there were any fourth-grade students available. Within a few minutes, three wide-eyed students entered the room. They had no idea why they had been recruited. Dana asked, "What is the one thing that if you were to do it better would improve your academics?" All three, almost instantaneously, identified the one thing they might do. They needed no coaching or prodding. They each knew immediately what the "one thing" was and weren't shy about sharing.

Students—younger or older—often know exactly what they can do to improve their scores. Then again, sometimes they need a little help. An obstacle for most students (and adults) is that they tend to shoot for goals beyond what is reasonable. According to Harvard's Tal Ben-Shahar, the best goals fall within a student's "stretch zone," which he defines as "the healthy median between their comfort and panic zones."[2] That zone will be different for each student, and they may need coaching around setting goals and being realistic.

Take Colby, for example. When Colby entered the fourth grade, he was already feeling defeated as a reader. He had struggled with reading from the first day he entered school, and he held a steady history of losing ground over the summer. Fourth grade was not going to be an exception.

Colby's teacher, Mrs. Brinson, invited all her students at the beginning of the year to set a reading WIG. Colby wrote: "To read better." Not too specific. And the fact was that Colby really didn't know how he could improve. He didn't even like to talk about reading scores.

He and Mrs. Brinson looked over his pretests and could see that what was most holding him back was his word accuracy. He would notice the beginning letters of a word and from there just take a guess at the word. Poor guesses were leading to his low reading scores.

Working together, they set Colby's goal to move up from a first-grade level (his X, where he was) in reading to a third-grade level (his Y, lag measure) by the end of the second grading period (his when). For Colby, it was an aggressive WIG, but Mrs. Brinson felt he could do it.

The class plan was to take a reading test every two weeks to see how each student was doing with reading. The results would provide each student with a frequent progress update. Colby and Mrs. Brinson also identified two lead measures or action steps for how the WIG could be achieved. Each day, Colby and Mrs. Brinson would read a few pages together out of his "Just Right" independent reading books during the class-designated reading time. He also earned a star that was put on a calendar just for reading with Mrs. Brinson (doing his action step) for that day. And he got an additional star if he did twenty minutes of reading at home at night. If Colby read with four or fewer errors, he earned a "bonus" star on his reading scoreboard.

Seeing the stars and progress on his reading graph and hearing Mrs. Brinson's steady encouragement motivated Colby to push himself even further. And by the end of the first marking period, Colby was on track to achieve his WIG by the end of the second term. With each success, Colby grew more confident in his reading, and Mrs. Brinson let him know how proud she was of him.

A student tracks progress toward his personal reading
WIG through use of a creative scoreboard.

It is important to note that sometimes the scores that are heralded most in schools are end-of-year scores. As vital as they are, end-of-year scores are far too far away for young students like Colby to even think about. Shorter-term goals with frequent progress monitoring are typically more motivating to them. Succeeding at multiple shorter goals is what eventually led Colby to achieve his WIG by the end of the second term and to brag to his peers about how he was a "leader of reading."

Before moving on to class or team WIGs, let's not overlook Mrs. Brinson. Mrs. Brinson had looked at her class's pretests and seen that only 42 percent of her students were at grade level in reading. She decided that her WIG—her "one thing that would have the greatest impact"—for the first term was to go from 42 percent of students reading at grade level to 50 percent by the end of the first term. She also set two action steps. One was to ensure that she set aside the time for her class to read daily for twenty minutes. She had been inconsistent in setting aside reading time the previous year due to distractions in her whirlwind. She was determined to get back into a consistent habit of twenty minutes. She figured her class had averaged twelve minutes of reading each day, so she set her WIG as going from averaging twelve to twenty minutes of reading each day until the end of the term.

Mrs. Brinson also saw in the pretest scores that Colby was by far her lowest-level reader. She knew that one of the rules of setting goals is not to set goals that someone else must achieve by changing their behavior. She instead had to focus on what she could do or change in her own actions so she could meet her goal. She needed to choose actions only she could take. She decided that one simple thing she could do was to sit by Colby during reading time and encourage him, point out what he was doing correctly, and identify the times when he was not seeing the whole word. If she could inspire Colby to get up to grade level, she would make a significant step toward reaching her academic WIG, as well as help Colby achieve his WIG. She kept her own reading chart for tracking all her students' reading progress every two weeks, and she could see that more students were indeed approaching grade level in reading, which she credited to consistently having her students read the twenty minutes each day. She ended up having two sets of accountability partners, one being her grade-level team that met each week as a professional learning community and the other being her students.

More on Colby's and Mrs. Brinson's WIGs later.

Team Goals

It was no secret among teachers and administrators at Colby's school that the school as a whole was struggling to get students up to grade level in reading. At the end of the previous year, only 36 percent of the school's students were reading at grade level. Something needed to be done. So each grade-level team was asked to set a WIG for increasing student success in reading.

The fourth grade had 44 percent of their students reading at grade level. As the fourth-grade teachers spoke about their possible WIG, the goal they chose was to go from 44 percent to 50 percent by the end of the second term.

But not all fourth-grade classes were at an equal place in their reading scores. Some had more challenging students and were below 40 percent. Other classes were already near 50 percent of students at grade level, so setting a WIG of 50 percent would be rather uninspiring for those higher-performing classes. So while the grade-level team set an overall WIG of 50 percent of students reading at grade level, each teacher needed to set a class WIG of their own.

Remember that Mrs. Brinson set her class WIG right at 50 percent. The teacher who had 50 percent of her students already reading at grade level set a WIG of 60 percent. Other teachers set lower WIGs. The hope was that by working together they could achieve an overall average of 50 percent.

Meeting as a grade-level PLC each week was their version of the weekly cadence. Each teacher talked about their class's progress, along with the challenges they were facing. They looked over the biweekly reading scores of each class, how individual students like Colby were doing, and discussed possible interventions. By helping each other, with each passing week they were coming closer to achieving their grade-level WIG.

Another thing that helped engage the students was the scoreboards that

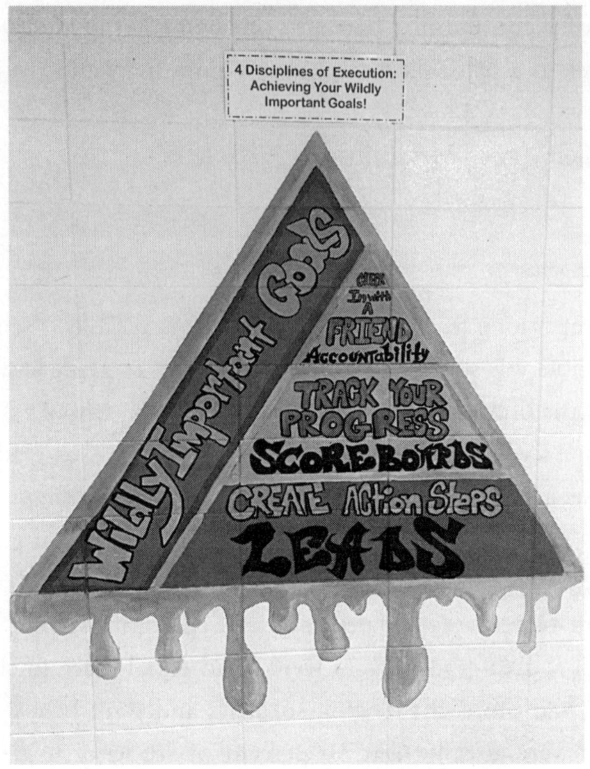

A dripping student interpretation adds a little fun to
the *4 Disciplines of Execution* model.

went up in the classrooms and hallway. Every two weeks the scoreboard in Mrs. Brinson's classroom and the hallway were updated. Each time a student in Mrs. Brinson's class tested at grade level, the scoreboard in her class inched closer to the 50 percent target on their scoreboard. There was a big pizza box at the end of the class scoreboard, along with reminders of what achieving grade level in reading could mean for students in life. Individual scores were kept confidential so as to maintain privacy and not to bring embarrassment to any one student.

Out in the hallway, there was a colorful scoreboard that had a movie and ice cream at the end of the grade-level scoreboard. Every two weeks, the students could see how much the grade level was progressing toward achieving its WIG.

Students and teachers work together to set and track
schoolwide WIGs and update scoreboards.

And in each classroom, students were making a game of it. They wanted to achieve the prize.

What has been skipped up to this point is an important and major part of setting a team WIG. It is that Mrs. Brinson did not set her class WIG by herself. She talked with the students about the need to get more of them reading at grade level. She described how reading was important for learning about any subject matter and how by reading better they would be doing better in all areas of academics. It was the "one thing that if they did it better would have greatest impact" on their academics. Perhaps the students did not suddenly become deeply committed to the idea, but it made enough sense to them that they agreed to go for it. Admittedly, offering an incentive helped get their commitment levels up: If their class achieved its WIG, there was a pizza party waiting for them. And if the entire grade achieved its WIG, there was ice cream and a full afternoon of movie-watching and fun added on. At that point, students like Colby began thinking not only about their class WIG and their personal WIG, but also about the entire grade-level WIG. They were even thinking about how they could help students in their class and the other fourth-grade classes achieve their WIGs.

One other step Mrs. Brinson took was to assign "leaders of reading." Each day, the leaders of reading would make a big check mark on their class calendar if they did their twenty minutes of reading. If they got to the end of the week and all five days of the week were checked, they celebrated that milestone with five extra minutes of recess, or whatever their celebration reward was determined for that week, which students would help Mrs. Brinson choose. And those student WIG leaders were not about to let Mrs. Brinson miss a day. In this way, Mrs. Brinson's WIG became the entire class's WIG, and one of her action steps became one of the class's lead measures. So perhaps you can see why the key word in setting a class or team WIG is "involvement." It was not something that was just dumped on the students. No involvement, no commitment.

Without getting too far ahead of ourselves, we might add here that we have seen students get pretty excited when they achieve their class- and grade-level WIGs. We were in one third-grade classroom when it was announced that they had hit their math WIG. Pandemonium erupted. The students were jumping up and down and celebrating together. It was as if a sports team had just won a championship. Likewise, we were also in a fifth-grade classroom that had a math WIG, and there were several students volunteering to mentor other students who were struggling with some math concepts. They wanted to help their peers achieve their WIG so the class as a whole could achieve its WIG. The volunteers appeared more excited about their peers achieving their WIGs than they were about achieving their own WIG. As for Colby, what truly elated him was the day his class met their WIG, partly as a result of him achieving his personal

WIG. He loved being one of the students who contributed to achieving the goal instead of one of the students holding it back. And you might imagine the thrill and cheering that went on when the date of the pizza, movie, and ice cream was announced for the entire grade level when they achieved their first-term WIG. Party time!

At Sallie Jones Elementary, a Legacy School in Florida, they like to have three-minute goal parties. When they achieve their WIGs, the lights are turned down, and students put on glow necklaces, play a favorite hit song, and dance to it. Every class can choose its own favorite reward.

At this point, what is left is to set a WIG and action steps for the second term.

Every Wildly Important Goal achieved deserves a grand, ringing celebration.

Aligned School Goals

What we have described thus far are the WIGs of one student (Colby), one teacher (Mrs. Brinson), and one grade-level team (the fourth grade). What might it look like if an entire school chose to pursue a WIG?

Well, that is exactly what Colby's school did. When the school administration examined the previous year's state exam scores, there was no question: The "one thing" they could do as a school was to increase the reading scores of their students. As a school, only 36 percent of students were reading at grade level. After talking about the various factors that were impacting students' reading scores, the teachers felt they could raise the number of student reading at grade level up to 55 percent by the end of the year. But it wasn't going to happen overnight, and it wasn't going to be easy.

While the whole school shared the same WIG, not everyone shared the same action steps. The grade-level teams would work in their PLCs to do their part at the class and grade levels. The principal and assistant principals committed to being in the classrooms for thirty minutes each day during the reading times of the various classrooms. It was not their typical role, but they wanted to be there reading with students, encouraging students, getting a general understanding of where individual students were at with their reading, and mostly supporting the teachers. They would also attend at least one grade-level team PLC each week to support and learn how they could help. They knew that if the school was to achieve its school WIG, it was going to happen one student at a time.

To make things easier for the grade-level teams, an existing staff meeting room was turned into a data room. It was designated as a private place reserved for the reading specialists, administrators, and grade-level teams to track and discuss the progress of each student. Each time students were tested for reading level, the reading specialist posted the scores in the data room so teachers would have easy access to them. The reading specialist attended each grade-level PLC at least twice a month to lend support. A fun and colorful schoolwide scoreboard showing the percentage of students reading at grade level filled a large bulletin board near the main entrance of the school so all could see. Everyone—students and adults—knew where the school was in its reading progress.

Students interact with the "Wall of Success" to track
achievements and celebrate progress.

In some cases, older students were assigned as reading mentors for younger students. Once a week, the older students would read with the younger students and cheer on their progress. For the older students, a group of assigned mentors from the nearby middle school visited them once a week and encouraged their reading.

After two years of implementing the *4 Disciplines* goal-setting process, fifth-grade teacher Julie indicated, "We are miles ahead from where we were five years ago. We as teachers used to set goals for kids and they didn't track them at all. Now students are accountable for setting and tracking their goals." Teacher Shannon added, "With students being responsible for their goals, they are much more interested when we ask, 'Is that a good choice of book? Will it help you toward your goal?' They aren't just trying to get a pizza party; they are trying to become better readers."

Much effort went into achieving the school's WIG, make no mistake about that. In the end, however, it was worth it. The school made its WIG of 55 percent of students reading at grade level. The next year it used the same *4 Disciplines* to reach 67 percent of students reading at grade level. Some classrooms exceeded their class WIGs; only a handful of classes came up short.

This is what is meant by "aligning for academic results." There was a clear school WIG. To meet the school WIG, each grade-level team had its own WIG, and each class, teacher, and student had their individual WIGs and clear action steps, scoreboards, and cadences of accountability. Granted, they might still be battling a whirlwind of tasks, but they were achieving the most wildly important tasks and making the greatest impact for their students. If one or two of their PIGs did not get achieved, that is okay.

The examples above center primarily on elementary school. The *4 Disciplines of Execution* apply equally as well to middle and high schools and to districts. For example, secondary schools are using the *4 Disciplines* to increase academic success for students across subject areas. By having students set individual goals related to the grades they are earning in their classes, the schools have increased student engagement and performance, as students regularly track lead measures like completing course assignments and studying their notes in the evenings. Students meet regularly for a few minutes in class to update their scoreboards and check in with their classmates on the progress they're making toward their target grades.

At the district level, districts like the Pella Community School District in Iowa come together to identify MRA (Measurable Results Assessment) targets that they want to improve across all their schools. Each school then sets its improvement targets around the common focus area and then plans for training and support throughout the year to achieve the goal. They make time during their district administrative meetings and walkthroughs for accountability sessions, and administer a mini-MRA using questions related to their specific targets to check on their progress each quarter.

Furthermore, several colleges and universities also apply the disciplines with success, with the help of our coaching services.

Nonacademic WIGs

Academics is just one area in which the *4 Disciplines of Execution* can be applied. In fact, numerous educators find it easier and more profitable to start by setting WIGs for improving the culture of the school or learning the leader-ship skills prior to working on academic WIGs.

So what are some nonacademic WIGs?

We love that one kindergartener set a WIG to go from not knowing how to blow a bubble using bubble gum to knowing how to blow a bubble by the end of the term. He was firmly committed to practicing daily. Some elementary school students set WIGs for getting better at a sport, playing a musical instrument, or learning a hobby. They are simple goals that give them experience with learning what a goal is and with feeling the joy and self-efficacy that come from achieving a goal. The more mature students become, the more mature their WIGs become.

We often encourage students to set one nonacademic WIG and one academic WIG, which increases the chances of them enjoying and being suc-cessful at one. WIGs can be set monthly, quarterly, or whatever length is deter-mined to be reasonable and age-appropriate.

Some secondary schools do WIGs as part of an advisory or homeroom pe-

Martin Petitjean Elementary's schoolwide scoreboard shows progress toward behavioral goals and celebrates collective achievement.

riod, a time when the teacher is responsible for those specific students, but the students are responsible for setting one personal and one academic WIG and meeting with a peer accountability partner independent of the teacher. They are largely left on their own to set and achieve the WIG, because with classes rotating every hour and so many students having varying goals, it would be impossible for secondary school teachers to work with all their students. Doing it this way ensures that each student has at least one teacher showing interest in their WIGs, if only on occasion.

At the classroom or school level, the *4 Disciplines* can also be applied to nonacademic goals. As Dr. Kim Cummins, principal of Martin Petitjean Elementary, a Legacy School in Rayne, Louisiana, observes, "Once teachers become familiar with the process and the value of goal setting, they realize how much easier it makes things. It applies to so many aspects of a school." In addition to academic WIGs, her school has applied the goal-setting process to:

- *Health and fitness.* Every month students set health and fitness goals, and track progress in their leadership notebook. Some track how many miles they walk during PE, with the goal of walking the equivalent of a marathon. Each mile they walk results in a paper shoe being placed on the class scoreboard. Student leaders also talk about goals for healthy eating as they review the food being served in the cafeteria that day.
- *Attendance.* Personal, class, and schoolwide attendance is tracked every day. When the school averages 97 percent attendance three days in a row, students get an extra five minutes of recess. Of the twenty-seven schools in their district, Petitjean ranks second in attendance and ten points higher than other schools in their immediate area, which is up significantly since they started setting and tracking goals, despite a high-risk population.
- *Speech.* The speech therapist has students set goals and track progress relative to each student's special need, such as articulation. Students keep progress charts in their leadership notebook and have shown markedly higher progress than students at equivalent schools in the area.

At a school in Michigan, the staff noticed recurring problems with hallways getting messy. The administrators turned the challenge over to the student lighthouse team. The student leaders set a WIG for achieving a "total cleanliness" score by the end of the term and made a rubric for how cleanliness would be measured. Students introduced the goal during the weekly Friday assembly and asked everyone to help. A scoreboard was posted in a main hallway for all to see. Students set the WIG and were the judges and scorekeepers. They also found creative ways to celebrate that motivated the students to commit to the WIG. Each week student leaders reported progress and suggested improvements during the Friday assembly. Once that goal was met for a consistent period of time, the student leaders decided to choose another WIG to work on.

Schools use the *4 Disciplines* to reduce discipline referrals, improve parent involvement, reduce tardiness, improve bus behavior, or to inspire other desired behaviors. Again, more in-depth coverage is found in the book by the same name.

We commonly illustrate the *4 Disciplines* in the shape of a mountain, as if the goal-setters are climbing from a place where they currently are (X) to a high place to where they want to be (Y), as shown below:

We conclude this portion of the chapter with an important point. It is difficult for teachers to get students to set, pursue, or achieve classroom or schoolwide goals without the teachers first connecting with students! According to Dr. John Shepard, principal of North Henderson High School in North Carolina, "Our greatest strength is the teacher-student connections we have built. Students will work hard for teachers who they feel truly believe in them." Half of his students speak English as second language, yet they consistently achieve some of the top academic growth in their state. In fact, the school is in the top 9 percent of all high schools in their state in academic growth. They talk with students about goals every week as part of their advisory meetings, but it would not go nearly as well if they did not first build the culture of the school and their relationships with students.

Indeed, we have had schools come to us and say, "We just want to do the *4 Disciplines*. We don't want to do all this other leadership and culture work. We just want to focus on the academics. It is where we have our greatest needs." And, admittedly, some schools have done it and succeeded. But most schools discover quickly that if the connections with students are not there, if the culture is not conducive to learning, if students are not empowered, then no academic intervention will stick for long. That is why *Leader in Me* sees leadership, culture, and academics as so closely interactive and integrated.

It is worth noting that the *4 Disciplines* are Habits 1, 2, and 3 in action. Habit 1: Be Proactive (take initiative to assume ownership for your achievements and outcomes). Habit 2: Begin with the End in Mind (be very clear about your purposes and priorities). Habit 3: Put First Things First (do the most important things—the big rocks—first). It is a deeper dive into the *7 Habits*.

Empower Learners

In addition to the *4 Disciplines*, aligning for academic results strongly encourages the use of three leadership tools. Each has the objective of turning as much ownership for learning over to the students as is developmentally appropriate. The three tools are: 1) leadership portfolios, 2) student-led conferences, and 3) empowering instruction.

Leadership Portfolios

One of the most powerful tools of *Leader in Me* is leadership portfolios. Leadership portfolios offer a single location for students to house their WIGs, track personal scoreboards, record leadership reflections, showcase their best work, and more. Most schools use a simple three-ring binder with tabs for the portfolios. Others create digital versions.

An impressive experience is when young students are given the chance to share their personal leadership portfolios with an adult and explain its contents. It quickly becomes clear that most students feel proud to share a little about who they are, their progress, and especially their celebrations.

A typical leadership portfolio will have a custom cover and at least five tabs:

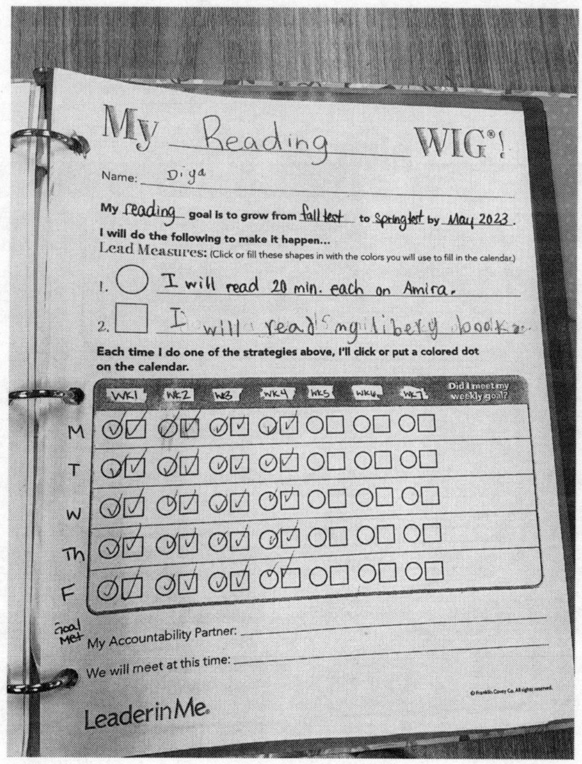

Students set, track, and reflect upon their individual goals in their leadership portfolio.

My Self, My Goals, My Learning, My Leadership, and My Celebrations. A guided tour of a student's leadership portfolio might look something like the following:

Cover. Students will typically create their own custom cover. It might consist of a hand-drawn or -painted work of art with their name on it, or if it is digital, it might consist of a photo of themselves or an image of a scene they relate with.

My Self. This is a place where students often place a copy of their mission statement, some fun facts about themselves, and maybe photos of them with their family or friends or doing favorite activities or hobbies.

My Goals. This is where students show evidence of their ongoing progress. It is where they keep and track their one to three WIGs. Typically, this is kept simple, perhaps two pages per WIG, with the first page indicating the WIG and the action steps (lead measures) the student wants to implement, and the second page containing scoreboards that track progress on the lead and lag measures.

A student shares her personal Mission Statement and Wildly Important Goals (WIGs) that she keeps inside her leadership portfolio.

My Learning. Here is where students show evidence of their progress in all areas of school. The more "kid-friendly" the graphs are, the more the students (especially young students) will be eager to fill them in with updates and share them with others. Typically, they will keep and track data from only two or three of their most important subject matter topics.

My Leadership. Roughly similar to a résumé, this is where students track what leadership roles they have fulfilled over a school year, both in the classroom and school. This includes service learning projects they have completed, speeches they have given, students they have mentored, or other ways they have been a leader. This is one of students' favorite places to insert photos of them being leaders.

My Celebrations. This is the place for students to house their best work. It is not meant to be a "junk drawer" where they keep every assignment, but a place where they display their proudest work, such as their highest scored assignments, their best accomplishments, or their favorite pieces of art. It can represent as many subject matter areas as the student wishes. It might also include nonacademic awards the student has earned or compliments they have received. It is a great place for teachers in specialty classes to contribute to the portfolios.

According to Dr. Kim Cummins, principal of Martin Petitjean Elementary, every student uses their leadership portfolio every day, starting on the first day of school. It is important that teachers feel ownership of what goes in their classroom's portfolios, and students need to feel ownership tracking and celebrating their progress. As one teacher told us, "The students are now a lot more aware of how they are doing in school than they ever were before."

Student-Led Conferences

An important leadership event that happens regularly in elementary schools is the traditional teacher-parent conference. Only in the case of *Leader in Me*, the conferences are student-led.

Many schools—including non–*Leader in Me* schools—have migrated to conducting student-led conferences, where, instead of a teacher or parent doing the talking, a student leads the discussion. In *Leader in Me*, students share with parents their WIGs and how they are progressing. They outline their strengths and ways they can improve. They walk their parents through their leadership portfolio. Parents and the teacher listen and ask questions. This keeps students in charge of their learning. It also has benefits for teachers, who, once they have the routine down, find it easier in terms of preparation. As a side benefit, since implementing the student-led format, the percentage of parents attending conferences at some schools has gone up as much as 20 percent. Students prod their parents to attend because they are eager to share their progress with them.

Principal Keli Sare notes, "We have a 90 percent participation rate of parents when students lead the conference, whereas if teachers run it far fewer parents come. That being said, it does not need to be parents who students present their leadership portfolios to. For schools where parent attendance is low, teachers look for other ways to provide the students a chance to share their progress and data. For example, at North Henderson High School, students create and present their portfolios as part of an English class assignment. They create them in a standardized digital format and present them to their peers during class. Other high school students have begun taking their portfolios to career fairs and internship supervisors."

One parent observed, "I was initially very skeptical about the concept of student-led conferences. But I quickly learned how valuable it is, because they feel so accountable and they sit with their teachers and explain to the parent what they've been doing and what goals they have set, and it really brings the accountability to them instead of the teacher." The parent added that it was "beautiful" that, despite being very young, students are "accountable for their choices at school, their learning, their grades. And they feel quite a sense of, 'This is on me, not on the teacher. It's not her fault if I mess up.'"

Empowering Instruction

The last tool is actually a set of instructional strategies for helping students take more responsibility for their in-class and out-of-class learning. It is an approach to education that puts the focus on learning rather than teaching. Three leveraged instructional habits bring the elements of the classroom together: trusting relationships, student-led learning, and collaborative planning and reflection.

Some teachers like to use the old traditional model for learning. They see themselves as the sages on the stages. They talk, and students listen. They present the facts, and students memorize the facts. They test students on the facts, and students recite the facts from memory. Not many teachers take that approach these days. Their aim is toward empowering students to take ownership of their own learning.

To empower students to take ownership of their learning requires using empowering instructional strategies. They ignite students' curiosities. They provide opportunities for students to investigate what lies beneath the facts and the ability to research and generate their own facts. They invite real-world connections. They give students choice and voice in terms of what and how they are learning. They do more than put bullet points on a slide and ask students to record and regurgitate the content. They recognize that different students have different learning styles. They understand that students appreciate variety in how they are taught.

Empowering students often requires that a blend of high-yield instructional strategies be used to help students reach their full learning capacities, strategies such as:

* asking questions that take students beyond yes/no answers;
* setting clear learning targets;
* using quality decision-making tools (graphic organizers);
* involving students in collaborative learning;
* asking for feedback on how teaching can be improved;
* using brain-based learning strategies;
* encouraging student-led self-assessments;
* optimizing digital learning;
* providing teach-to-learn opportunities;
* implementing problem-based learning; and
* offering freedom to explore and innovate (e.g., Genius Hour).

Of course, there are many more strategies for empowering students to take ownership of their learning. *Leader in Me* does not prescribe which strategies are the best for any given set of students. That is up to the teachers. What it does suggest is that students learn more and achieve more when they are engaged in the learning process, which requires much more than entertainment. It involves students becoming leaders of their own learning.

In Summary

A teacher reported: "We've been doing the *4 Disciplines* consistently over the last four years. As a school, we're now at the highest percentage as a school of students reading on or above grade level that we've ever been." And another said, "Students are absolutely learning greater self-responsibility from this because they're tracking goals, setting goals, learning how to manage their time."

Battle Ground Elementary was an F-rated school when it started *Leader in Me*. In one year, the teacher turnover rate dropped from 16 percent to 3 percent. Teachers who were skeptical and wanted to quit or retire wanted to stay, every student's test scores rose, and the school missed becoming a B-rated school by only three points. They, too, credit much of their success to putting the *4 Disciplines* into action.

And so we see the benefits of educators and students breaking apart their whirlwinds and focusing their efforts on the wildly important. Nevertheless, in concluding this chapter, let's ensure that under no circumstance should a student be made to feel that a goal—not even a Wildly Important Goal, or any academic test score—is of more worth than the student.

Are academics important? Absolutely!

Are class, school, and district academic goals important? Absolutely!

Yet none are of more worth than the uniquely individual student, goal or no goal.

So to this point, we have examined what educators in *Leader in Me* schools are doing to address the three common challenges: leadership, culture, and academics. Now, before moving on to the next chapter, let's pause and take a big-picture look at what is ahead.

Chapter 6, "Bringing it Home," describes how schools involve families in *Leader in Me* and how families can benefit from bringing the same principles home. Chapter 7, "Engaging the Community," shares examples of how and why communities are getting involved. Chapter 8, "Keeping It Alive," shares vital insights for sustaining *Leader in Me* over time and for "raising the bar" year after year. Lastly, Chapter 9, "Ending with the Beginning in Mind," is a reminder of how *Leader in Me* inspires students and adults to see themselves as leaders and to live life in crescendo.

A student presents schoolwide academic and attendance
goals with a visiting guest at Leadership Day.

6

Bringing It Home

Some of the most rewarding accounts of what *Leader in Me* can produce are happening in students' homes. Consider two examples.

The first comes from Canada, where a father showed up at a *Leader in Me* school with his son. The son had been diagnosed with a cognitive delay and oppositional defiance, and the father had been told the school had a culture that could possibly help him. He flexed his bulging muscles as he stated, "I want my son enrolled. Today!"

The son was admitted and was learning the *7 Habits* with all the other students the next day. As the weeks progressed, the son would occasionally bring home an assignment to teach a *7 Habits* concept to a parent. He taught his dad.

A few months went by, and the father attended a parent night. During a question-and-answer period, he stood and asked permission to say something. "What this school is teaching my son has changed my life," he said. "Keep doing what you are doing." He then sat down.

At a later time, the father revealed to the principal that years earlier he had been caught with drugs and arrested. While awaiting a court date, he fled and went into hiding. He eventually met a woman, and they had a child—the son. The dad found a job and began living a productive, drug-free life, yet he could never shake the worry that law enforcement officials were one step behind him.

The father went on to say that the lessons his son taught him about being proactive, about taking responsibility for one's actions, about having goals in life, and about putting first things first had pricked his conscience. They inspired him to want to set things right so he could relax and be the kind of dad he wanted to be. Ultimately, he contacted authorities and turned himself in. Then, speaking of his son, the father added, "This boy's my hero!"

As it turned out, a sympathetic judge examined the evidence of what the father had done during his years in hiding. It included a letter from the school principal emphasizing the importance of the father's relationship with his son. To the father's relief, the judge issued a ruling that allowed him to avoid prison time, stay at home, and pay penitence in other ways. It all started with the son teaching the *7 Habits* to his father.

The second story involves a teacher. Her school's full staff was going through the *7 Habits* workshop together, and at each break she would approach the facilitator and say, "Let me make sure I understand this habit correctly." She would then ask clarifying questions. Her intent was to go home and teach the habits to her family.

A year later, the same facilitator was visiting that same school and happened to meet that same teacher in a hallway. He asked how things were going with teaching the habits to her students. "Oh," she responded rather casually, "it's going okay." The facilitator was a little disappointed with her low-key response. But then he remembered the teacher's quest to teach the habits to her family. He asked, "What about your family? How did it go with teaching the habits to your family?" The teacher's instant response came with no words, just tears.

She explained that at the time she was going through the *7 Habits* training, her family was going through hell at home. Her two teenage sons were messing up their lives. Her husband was out of work and battling depression. Divorce was a constant topic and threat. So, as she was going through the *7 Habits* training, all she could think about was how much her family needed the *7 Habits*. And that is why she was determined to take the habits home.

The teacher did end up teaching the habits to her family. Together, they covered one habit per night. A year later, all the teacher could say through her tears was that the *7 Habits* saved her family, saved her marriage, and perhaps saved her husband's life.

It thrills us to say that we hear many similar stories coming from homes around the globe. Some of the most humorous examples are when young elementary students use the habits to teach a parent or older sibling how to be more effective.

The Home and School Relationship

No two families are alike. They come in all shapes and sizes. Each is unique. No family is perfect.

For better or worse, students bring influences from home to school that impact the culture of a school and classroom, which in turn impacts the students' yearning for learning. This is why it is best when teachers and parents are united in their efforts to create a positive learning environment. Karen L. Mapp of Harvard University's Graduate School of Education reports that when the home and school staff work together, "students earn higher grades, perform better on tests, and have better social skills and behaviors. They also have a greater likelihood of finishing high school and continuing on to higher education."

Adults likewise carry remnants from home to school each day. What deeds were done or parting words were spoken in their homes that morning can potentially make or break teachers' moods and actions for that entire day or longer. Any stress, conflict, or ineffectiveness that adults bring from home to school can impact their readiness to perform on the job. The better things are at home, the better things go at school.

In the same way that home can impact what happens at school, the school can have significant impact on what happens at home. Students spend more than six hours a day at school. The friends they meet, the teachers to whom they are assigned, the opportunities and responsibilities they are given, and the knowledge they attain all have the potential to wriggle their way into the home—again, for better or worse.

Educators do not want to be in the business of telling parents how to raise their families any more than they want parents telling them how to run their classroom. One principal in a middle-class neighborhood told us that before *Leader in Me*, she had parents trying to *direct* everything that happened at the school. Now they are asking, "How can we *support* what you are doing?" That alone made a big culture difference in her school. Another parent said, "I now look at the school in a much more positive light than I did before *Leader in Me*. It's sort of like we're all on the same team and we're all striving to understand each other."

This chapter shares a few success stories of how families and schools are working together to make life a little easier for everyone. Note that we said "easier," not "easy." It explores:

* Teaching the *7 Habits* at Home
* Creating a Leadership Culture at Home
* Achieving Family Goals at Home
* Engaging Families at School

Teaching the 7 Habits at Home

It is a source of amusement to hear about parents who come to their child's school and ask with puzzled looks on their faces, "What are you teaching my child? He keeps saying things like, 'Momma, can't we synergize around this?' Or 'Why don't we ever sharpen the saw and do something fun?'" It is a good sign that students are taking the habits home.

There are several ways to inform parents about the *7 Habits*. Common methods include:

Letters Home. Most schools send a letter home prior to or at the beginning of a school year to inform parents about *Leader in Me*. Typically, it is as simple as a two-sided note. On the front page is an overview of the major strategies and benefits of *Leader in Me*. On the back is a summary of the *7 Habits*. Parents may choose to place the *7 Habits* summary in a visible spot where family members will see it often.

Welcome Packets. For new students who arrive during the year, schools create a packet with photos and examples of what the school is doing to implement *Leader in Me*. Success stories, testimonials, and answers to frequently asked questions are also included.

Newsletters. Many schools and classrooms send home weekly, monthly, or quarterly newsletters. A portion of the newsletters are set aside to highlight one of the habits or to share a success story. Sometimes it is as simple as a weekly or monthly quote.

Digital Messages. Some schools maintain a social media account, an app, or a website that offers updates on all things related to *Leader in Me*, including photos, calendared events, or fun traditions. Similarly, many teachers like to send a text message to parents once a week communicating what *7 Habits* topic or other leadership principle is being studied that week.

Book Library. Some schools set up a family library for parents to check out books and audios related to *Leader in Me*, including:

- *The 7 Habits of Highly Effective People*
- *The 7 Habits of Highly Effective Teens*
- *The 7 Habits of Happy Kids*
- *The 7 Habits of Highly Effective Families*[1]
- *Trust and Inspire*[2]
- *Teacher Believed in Me*[3]

Each book is a valuable resource for parents to acquaint themselves with the habits and other leadership principles. One school in Illinois found grant money to purchase a copy of *The 7 Habits of Happy Kids* for every family and asked them to read it and discuss the chapter questions with their children. New families are also given a copy of the book upon registering their child.

Students Teaching the Habits to Their Families

Our favorite way for families to learn about the *7 Habits* is for students to teach the *7 Habits* at home. Students can use the same methods their teachers use—namely, direct lessons, integrated approaches, and modeling.

Direct Lessons. One effective way for parents to learn about the habits is for students to take assignments home to teach the habits to parents and siblings. Such assignments typically contain a short lesson followed by a discussion of how the family can apply the habit.

Some parents, including teachers, prefer to teach the *7 Habits* to their families. At the beginning of this chapter, we cited the example of the teacher who took her *7 Habits* training manual home and taught the concepts to her family. Her approach was exactly what her struggling family needed.

Integrated Approaches. Some parents find ways to integrate the habits into activities or tasks that are already being done in the home. The simplest way for this to happen is for parents to use the *7 Habits* language: "I'm sorry, I should have sought first to understand." Or "Hey, does anyone want to sharpen the saw with me? I need a break, so I'm going for a walk." The more young people hear the language being applied in authentic situations by their parents, the more practical understanding of the habits they will have.

Parents who read with their children can spot one or more of the habits in most any book they are reading. Many movies or newspaper articles also include examples of the use (or abuse) of a habit and the resulting consequences. Parents can share stories from family histories that support a leadership principle, or they can go to places on family vacations or do other activities that somehow reinforce leadership skills and principles. Or parents can take a child to meet a friend, relative, or neighbor who has exhibited excellence in a particular talent or field and ask them questions about what it means to be a leader. If a child likes a particular sport or hobby, parents might ask them who the leaders in that field are and what makes them a leader.

Inserting a brief "life lesson" during a dinner conversation is another opportunity to integrate a *7 Habits* lesson into a general conversation. Such lessons may need to be restricted to thirty-second sound bites—and that is okay. In fact, one parent sends her teens inspiring texts during the day, followed by a "Luv u" or a compliment. They just need to not go overboard in their efforts, or else their teens are going to start saying, "Don't *7 Habits* me!"

Modeling. If ever there is a place where the world needs fewer critics and more models, it is in the home. Homes are in constant need of modeling and remodeling.

Often, it is the students who are doing the modeling. One dad was surprised when his first-grade son began washing dishes without being prompted. He asked, "What are you doing?" The son responded, "I'm being proactive and helping without being asked." The father, a corporate executive, said, "You don't even know what the word 'proactive' means." At that, the father sat in awe as his son taught him all about Habit 1.

Young Lizzie collaborates with her siblings to create a vision board as a way of applying leadership principles at home.

One parent sent a note to the principal that read:

Today was my daughter's second day at your school. She is a third grader. When we arrived home, she and her sister began to argue. After less than ten seconds my daughter said, "I am not going to argue with you. I am going to be proactive, not reactive. We can think of a win-win solution." This was after only two days! I could not believe it. Thank you!

Another parent wrote:

One night I came home and my daughters were busy cleaning their rooms—an event not too common without prodding. I kept asking, "What's going on here?" The girls said, "We're being proactive. We're synergizing. We're doing win-win." They were doing it all on their own. The 7 Habits are now integrated in a lot of our home activities. We ask, "What are our first things?" and then we focus on doing those things. It has reduced a lot of stress in our home. I learned these concepts as a manager. I wish I had learned them as a child.

Similarly, we chuckled when hearing about the father who was driving home from an event when a driver cut him off. The father's temper and nostrils flared as he shouted at the offending driver. At that point, his elementary school–age daughter spoke up in her sweet voice from the back seat. "Daddy, I wonder how we could have been a little more proactive in that situation."

Creating a Leadership Culture at Home

The *Leader in Me* culture at school provides a valuable template to consider when thinking about how to create an effective culture at home. This includes:

- The Physical Environment
- The Social-Emotional Environment

- Leadership Events
- Shared Leadership

The Physical Environment

The main question to ask in designing the physical environment of a home is, "What do the walls communicate about the worth and potential of each person who lives here?"

One of our consultants was displaying photos of school hallway displays and asking the teachers, "What do your school walls communicate to students?" No sooner had he said those words than the thought crossed his mind, "What do the walls of my home say to my children?" Before long, the consultant and his wife had removed some of the nice store-bought wall hangings they had mounted on a large wall and turned it over to their children to redecorate. What their children wanted was a bulletin board full of photos of fun family memories. Once the board was completed, the children were quick to take their friends to see it. It was their wall. Unlike the old store-bought items, it was full of memories.

Teens like looking in mirrors, so putting the *7 Habits* or other inspiring messages on their mirror is a good option. One parent worked with her boys to plaster their entire bathroom with leadership quotes and thoughts. "They're all going to spend time in there eventually," she said, "so they might as well be thinking positive thoughts."

Another parent dedicated one room of their home as a children's art gallery of sorts. All the walls and shelves contained the colorful arts and crafts her children had created. Her children felt most at home in that room.

Another parent was open with us about her drug problem. She truly wanted to change. So she placed a list of the *7 Habits* on her bathroom mirror and read them out loud to herself every morning. "I needed them as a daily reminder, even more than my kids needed them," she said.

The founder of a large holding company removed a painting from one of the walls in his home and replaced it with a photo of his father. "That photo is my personal mission statement," he said. "I want to be the type of father and leader he was."

The Social-Emotional Environment

The social-emotional environment of a home is largely determined by what is heard and what is felt.

Home environments bring out the best and worst in people. Much of it starts with the language that is spoken—what is heard. Is it mostly affirming or condescending? How is each individual respected, including the child who tests parents the most? How do family members work together to solve problems?

As cautions, when using the language of leadership at home:

- *Don't* use the *7 Habits* to criticize. If all a child hears is "You're not being proactive . . ." or "Why didn't you put first things first like I told you to . . . ?" chances are they will develop an allergic reaction to the language of the habits.
- *Do* use the language as a positive affirmation or healer. For example, "I was so impressed with how proactive you were." "I was amazed at how you put first things first." "I'm sorry, I didn't seek first to understand." Or "I apologize. That was a total win-lose choice on my part."

Think of the *7 Habits* as tools to keep in the family toolbox for when times get tough or things become broken. One of our colleagues, Chad Smith, likes to tell people that "the *7 Habits* are at their best when they have a problem to solve." And nowhere does that appear to be more true than in family settings. Families can use the *7 Habits* to address all kinds of challenges, including planning a vacation or solving a conflict. In fact, the next time a conflict or disagreement arises with a family member or partner, consider the following suggestions as possible action steps for helping to resolve the issue.

Key Actions to Conflict Resolution

Be Proactive

- Gain control of your emotions. Pause until tempers cool.
- Stop and think. What is the *right* thing to do?
- Focus on your circle of influence, what is within your control.
- Take responsibility for your actions rather than making excuses. Apologize.

Begin with the End in Mind

- Choose your battles. Do not contend over matters that have no relevance to what is truly important.
- Focus on what you want your relationship with the family member to "feel" like once the disagreement is resolved.
- Tell the person from the start that you value them and want to make things right.

Put First Things First

- Act on conflicts in a timely manner; do not allow them to fester or grow.
- Be true to your values.
- Avoid saying things you will later regret.

Think Win-Win

- Balance courage with consideration. Be considerate of others, and don't be afraid to express your own feelings.
- Make meaningful "deposits" in the person's Emotional Bank Account. Forgive.
- Seek mutually beneficial outcomes. Say no to outcomes that will help you but not help the other person.
- Avoid comparing a child to other children.

Seek First to Understand, Then to Be Understood

- Listen with undivided attention. Say no to television, cell phones, or other interferences when talking things out.
- Listen with your ears, eyes, and heart until the person feels understood.
- Be open to feedback; correct inaccurate feedback.
- Communicate your feelings without attacking the other person.

Synergize

* Be humble. A temper gets people into trouble; pride keeps them there.

* Let the best solution win. Yours might not always be the best.

* Look for third alternatives, solutions that are better than either party has suggested.

* Seek out people who might have a more objective or educated view, and who might provide a better solution than those who are directly involved.

Sharpen the Saw (the great conflict preventer)

* Get rest, exercise, and eat right. Fatigue, poor nutrition, and stress feed conflict.

* Take preventive actions. Build good relationships in calm times.

* Learn and practice stress reduction strategies.

* Learn about basic human psychology to understand why a family member might think or behave in certain ways and at different stages of life.

* Build your self-confidence. Avoid entering conflicts feeling vulnerable and weak.

One way to create a favorable social-emotional environment in a home is to create a family mission statement. Our company works with thousands of organizations around the world. Most have a mission statement or values statement. Yet when it comes to families—the most important organization in the world, in our opinion—mission statements are relatively rare.

Several schools encourage families to create a family mission statement. Steps families can consider when building a mission statement include:

First, *explore what your family is about*. Involve family members in asking questions such as:

* What is the purpose of our family?
* What kind of family do we want to become?
* What are our family's highest-priority goals?
* What are our talents, gifts, and abilities?
* When are we the happiest?
* What do we want our home to look like, feel like, and sound like?
* What makes us want to be at home?

- How can we be of most help to each other?
- To what will we commit to saying no?

Initially, children may resist answering such questions. But in a high-trust situation, most children will warm up and even come to like discussing such issues, especially if their opinions are valued. They like to have a say in family matters.

Second, *write it down*. Some families cut out pictures from magazines to make a family mission statement collage. Some make up a song. But eventually it helps to get it in writing. Written mission statements do not need to be lengthy or perfectly written. Tips include: 1) Be practical. Write it as though you intend to live it. 2) Consider all four basic needs: physical, social-emotional, mental, and spiritual—thinking about the whole child, the whole family. 3) Keep the language and ideas at a level that can be understood by all. 4) Don't try to get it perfect. Start with a rough draft.

Three, *use it*. Once a draft is written, try living up to the mission statement,

A student confidently shares and discusses data about her
academic progress during a student-led conference.

especially as a parent. Use the mission statement to make decisions. Plan specific activities that reinforce the mission statement. A mission statement is meant to inspire, not to be a rule book. Use it to course-correct as needed. A family may even want to set one or two WIGs that relate to their mission statement. Clearly state the WIG. Identify key behavior changes and lag measures. Create a scoreboard. Meet on occasion to assess progress and hold each other accountable. Celebrate. Remember, highly effective families come from proactive, intentional planning and goal setting. They do not result from chance.

Leadership Events

One parent stated, "As good as we felt our family was before we were introduced to the *7 Habits*, we are even better now."

Dr. John (Stephen R. Covey's brother) and Jane Covey have devoted a significant portion of their lives to teaching the *7 Habits* to families from all around the world. They identify three family events that generate high outcomes from making small investments of time. They all start with the word "one."

One meal together. Busy schedules make it easy for a family to live in the same house and never communicate, like passengers in an airport passing each other with no meaningful interactions. One meal a day together can bond a family. It may last only twenty minutes, but even that is ample time for parents to hear things that need to be heard, to share a positive idea, or to communicate a child's worth and potential. Before sitting down to eat, a parent can pause and think: "How can I best use this time to build family ties and trust?" Mealtimes can provide nutrients for family members' minds, hearts, and spirits—in addition to what it does for their bodies.

One night per week family time. Setting aside one night (or day) each week as family time makes room for more meaningful interactions. It is time to do something fun, work on a project, or do service as a family. Some find it helpful to schedule it for the same night every week so children learn to plan on it—it becomes a family habit. When it is not scheduled, chances of it happening are always in jeopardy.

One-on-one conversations. Every child is unique, and each deserves personal attention. Young children thrive on one-on-one time, whereas teens are prone to resist it, particularly if it feels "planned" or they sense it is an "I'll fix you" session. One busy father with a large family made it a habit to wash dishes with each child on an assigned night. His teens never turned down the help, nor did they know it was dad's built-in way of ensuring he was spending weekly one-on-one time with each child. "How's school going? What fun things are you learning? How is [friend's name] doing?" A mother designated brushing-teeth time as one-on-one time with her young children. She committed to saying only positive things about them during that time. Parents are busy, children are busy, and so sometimes one-on-one time never happens—unless it is planned.

Like these three "one" events identified by Dr. John and Jane Covey, any family activity or project can be turned into a family leadership event. Even driving a child to school can be a one-on-one leadership event. They are opportunities to build a family culture, create a vision of the future, and establish trust while doing normally occurring tasks.

Shared Leadership

As at school, children can be given opportunities to be leaders at home by giving them worthwhile responsibilities to lead and valuing their opinions.

Most parents post job charts or give regular assignments to children. In addition to those basic and necessary chores, children can be given opportunities to take on meaningful assignments that build skills, raise confidence, and demonstrate trust. One father had his eleven-year-old son ask to replace the garbage disposal that had broken on their kitchen sink. "No way" was the dad's first thought. "Why not?" was his second. "It will give us time together, and I can teach him how to do it right when he gets it wrong." The father then watched as the son did the entire job correctly without help—a real confidence builder for the son and the father. The son felt pride in his work and that he had done something of value.

Some parents like to give their children the responsibility to plan a family activity, or even a family trip. By entrusting them with such important responsibilities, parents are communicating to their children that they have worth and potential. They like that feeling.

Children also like the feeling of having their voices and opinions heard. They have opinions about how chores are to be done, about plans for the week, about what kind of meals to eat, about consequences for misbehavior, and so forth. Some parents may "panic" at the thought of turning certain decisions over to their children, but when mutual trust is present in the relationship, the children will often surprise parents with their ideas and solutions. We recall one set of parents who had planned for years and saved money to make a big trip to a famous amusement park. It was all part of their yearslong sacrifice for their children. When they announced the surprise to their children, the children seemed less than enthusiastic. "We'd rather do our traditional camping trip with our cousins," they said. Had the parents involved their children earlier in the decision, the parents would have saved themselves years of scrimping and used the money instead for several small family activities over the years.

Children want and deserve opportunities to be leaders in the home and to have their opinions valued.

Engaging Families at School

Another way to expose parents and families to the *7 Habits* and *Leader in Me* is to invite them to be a part of the school by hosting family events and inviting parents to volunteer.

Hosting Family Events

Many schools already host family events, so most often this is a matter of finding ways to integrate the *7 Habits* or other leadership principles into those existing events. Consider a few examples:

Back-to-School Night. Most elementary and several secondary schools host back-to-school evenings for parents prior to the start of school. Those nights are good opportunities to inform parents about *Leader in Me* and to give them a preview of the types of things their children will be learning and experiencing.

7 Habits **Nights.** Some schools set aside a special parent afternoon or evening for a one-to-two-hour overview of the *7 Habits*. The goal is to help parents become familiar with the language and basic concepts. Some offer it in multiple languages.

Cultural Nights. Especially in schools with varying cultural populations, a great way to involve families is to celebrate the various cultures. Examples include international folk dancing performances, cultural cooking demonstrations, playing cultural games, or hearing from global guests.

Donuts with Grown-Ups. Numerous elementary schools have the tradition of inviting dads or moms (or even grandparents) to read with their children on a designated day. Cunningham Elementary in Waterloo, Iowa, has turned the event into a leadership event. It invites dads (or an uncle, cousin, grandpa, or other male role model) to read with their children about someone who is a leader. Dads then spend time telling their child what characteristics they feel are important to being a leader and describing the leadership characteristics they see in their child. The donuts are merely a tantalizing sideshow.

Parent Leadership Day. As described previously, some schools hold Leadership Days and large audiences of fellow educators show up to learn about the school. Many schools will often invite parents or caregivers a day or two prior to the big event to be a dress-rehearsal audience. Parents and grandparents get to see their children perform talents and share their leadership portfolios.

Parent Classes. Several schools or districts offer opportunities for parents to experience *The 7 Habits of Highly Effective Families* workshop. This can be done in a single day, such as on a weekend day, or spread over a period of one-hour evenings.

In short, virtually any typical school event that involves families—concerts, plays, field days, etc.—can be turned into opportunities for families to become familiar with the habits. Some parents have told us how their child began kindergarten already knowing the *7 Habits* as a result of having attended family activities at the school and seeing their older siblings teach the habits or be leaders.

When holding *7 Habits* events for parents or families, a lesson can be learned from what happened at Janson Elementary, a Legacy School in Rosemead, California. One year, the staff taught a *7 Habits* class for parents, and forty parents showed up. It was a tremendous success. The next year they decided to hold a night for students to teach families the habits. Each grade level was assigned a habit to teach using speeches, songs, skits, art, or whatever method they chose. As the evening drew near, the principal at the time, Gabriel Cardenas, grew nervous. The chatter he was hearing made him worry that he might not be able to fit all the guests into his small gym. So he asked the minister at a church next door for permission to use his facility. The church held eight hundred people, but it was still too small to hold the crowd that showed up! The lesson is that if an in-depth discussion about the *7 Habits* is the goal, then small classes for parents work well. If broad exposure is the desired outcome, turn the event over to students.

Families and students jointly participate in a school event, thereby strengthening community connections beyond the classroom.

Engaging Parents as Volunteers

Another way to introduce parents to *Leader in Me* is to invite them to volunteer, to get involved.

When a student named Kyle arrived at Principal Cris Edwards's school, he had a speech disorder. He couldn't make sounds properly and was nonverbal. He had a speaking device but did not like to use it. He would have outbursts. He was always worried other students would make fun of him. At first his mother tried to protect him from being given leadership assignments. But with the principal's encouragement, he started taking on small roles, and it built his confidence to the point that before he left the school, he became a master of ceremonies for Leadership Day. His mother, seeing what *Leader in Me* was doing for her son, decided that instead of resisting *Leader in Me*, she would get involved. She volunteered with the band and eventually became known as the band mom, even after Kyle had graduated and moved on. She and Kyle literally found their voices at the school. It changed the trajectory of their family life.

Students at A.B. Combs fine-tune their greeting and leadership skills as they welcome guests to their school.

Opportunities for parent volunteers to become involved include:

* Inviting one parent per month to share personal experiences related to what they have learned about leadership in their careers. One parent, for example, taught students what firefighters need to know about leadership.
* Organizing mini job fairs where students rotate from parent to parent learning about different careers and how leadership is important in those careers.
* Having parents volunteer their skills to help students create art displays, write songs, or write plays that integrate the habits.
* Asking parents to teach students how to manage real-life projects. For example, one parent who was an architect led a fifth-grade class through the process of designing their ideal classroom. They began with the end in mind by making real blueprints. Another parent, a graphic designer, taught a class how to design amazing art for their classroom using professional equipment.

Parent volunteers can be responsible for creating a *Leader in Me* welcome packet for new families, for recruiting and scheduling parent volunteers, for helping the librarian identify books with *7 Habits* connections, and so forth. Several schools create a parent lighthouse team that works with students to plan and arrange leadership events for students and families. The right parents can lift a lot of effort from staff members' shoulders while bringing a variety of new talents. And though most parents are busy, most of them have a hard time turning down the opportunity to be recognized as Parent Leader of the Day.

Go Easy

Sometimes parents come out of *7 Habits* activities pumped up and ready to change the world. They want every one of their family members to get excited about the *7 Habits*. They are disappointed when some family members don't immediately follow their lead.

If you are a parent, a few tips for engaging family members include:

Make a Plan. Look over the suggestions in this chapter and choose a few activities or ideas to work on as a starting place. Spread them out over a year's time so that you do not try to do too much at once. If you ever feel your plan is too slow-paced or overambitious, adjust. A yearly plan often provides a sense of balance.

Learn to Say No! Examine your current family calendar to see if there are less important things that can be removed. If so, say no to them and replace them with more worthwhile activities. Be honest. Are there things you are currently doing that, in the grander scheme of things, are a waste of time? Upon honest examination, big blocks of time that are habitually spent watching television or playing video games may turn out to be time fillers. Replace them with mind fillers.

Students welcome community visitors with a musical performance, showing that everyone can in some way be a leader.

Keep It Simple. Remember how teachers say, "This is not one more thing. It is a better way of doing what we are already doing." That is also a good way to approach *Leader in Me* at home. Look at what is already being done and add a leadership twist to it. If you are already eating dinner as a family, use the time to intentionally build relationships rather than to discuss minutiae or argue. If you are already exercising regularly, take a child on a walk and use the time to tell stories of people you know who exhibit leadership qualities. In other words, keep doing what you are already doing—just do it through a new leadership lens.

Have Fun. If you feel tensions rising because your son is ruining your great plan to discuss a habit as a family, then consider backing off. If you are irritated because your daughter is singing away while you are trying to get her to listen

This family engages with the 7 Habits of Happy Kids board game, reinforcing leadership principles at home.

to *The 7 Habits of Highly Effective Teens* audio, hold your tongue. The suggestions in this chapter are intended to make things at home better, not to start a war. Learning about leadership and the habits is meant to be fun, not one more homework assignment.

Start with Yourself. Win your own battles of personal and interpersonal effectiveness first, then help others win theirs. The only thing we can control is ourselves, so why not start there? As you model and find success in living the habits, family members will be more inclined to follow your lead.

Leadership in the home sets the pattern and foundation for leadership in society, including in schools. So why not begin at home, starting with a simple plan?

7

Engaging the Community

"The research is abundantly clear," says Michael Fullan. "Nothing motivates a child more than when learning is valued by schools and families/community work together in partnership. . . . These forms of involvement do not happen by accident or even by invitation. They happen by explicit strategic intervention."[1]

Our favorite part of that opening statement is that the partnerships happen as a result of "explicit strategic intervention." They don't fall into place by accident. They happen by design.

Whoever originated the proverb "It takes a village to raise a child" was observant and correct. It can also be observed that "It takes workforce-ready students to sustain a village." It is an ecosystem.

Yet the relationship between schools, communities, and families has not always been synergistic. Many educators will confess that they dislike business-people who meddle in their affairs. At the same time, some business leaders are frustrated by the lack of skills they see in the coming workforce.

The good news is that from our vantage point the relations between schools and community partners are improving. They are combining their strengths for the good of students and finding harmonious ways to supply students with the workforce readiness skills they need to successfully launch into society after graduation. And they should. After all, happy, well-prepared, and successful students lead to happy, well-prepared, and successful citizens and workers at all levels of society.

For the purposes of this chapter, we keep it local and describe some of the best practices that districts, community groups, and individual philanthropists have contributed to the success of *Leader in Me*.

District Engagements

Thousands of schools have embarked on their *Leader in Me* journey with little to no district or community involvement. Those schools have examined what it takes to be a successful *Leader in Me* school, and they have made an intentional investment and commitment to implement the process on their own. And most produce tremendous outcomes.

However, schools that embark "on their own" miss out on the synergy that can happen among educators from the various schools within a district that implements *Leader in Me*, as well as the economies of scale that can occur. At present, there are over five hundred districts implementing *Leader in Me* in the US alone. Within those districts, teachers and administrators exchange ideas and share resources. Many districts certify their own coaches to train all staff in the *7 Habits* and facilitate other *Leader in Me* workshops. When a student, teacher, or administrator moves from one school to another within the district, there is a level of consistency. So there are benefits and synergies that come from multiple schools within a district participating in *Leader in Me*.

Districts also have the benefit of being able to scaffold *Leader in Me* content and objectives across the elementary, middle, and high school levels. For example, several districts emphasize *learning* the *7 Habits* in their elementary schools, *applying* the habits in their middle schools, and *leading* the school—having greater voice—in their high schools. It is a coordinated district strategy.

Districts tend to have greater leverage in engaging the full community than individual schools do. Whereas individual schools typically have the connections to obtain financial support and resources from a handful of local businesses, districts are more likely to have better connections to engage the entire community. To make it happen and achieve the districts' desired results, the districts organize individuals as internal coaches. They have the responsibility for ensuring that the training and quality of implementation are maintained and sustained throughout the participating schools in their districts, while at the same time empowering schools to make it their own.

So, yes, individual schools can have a great experience when implementing *Leader in Me* on their own—and many do—but there are many tangible benefits to having the partnership and support of a district. Furthermore, when the entire district is involved, the leadership principles being taught have the benefit of being applied and modeled at all levels of the district. It provides a common culture and a common language that is spread throughout the district.

As with schools, every district will implement according to their own needs and capacities. Each makes it their own. While it is not reasonable to describe all five hundred of the various districtwide implementations in these few pages, what follows are a few examples.

One of the first districts to gradually implement *Leader in Me* was the Pryor Public Schools district in Oklahoma. Fred Sordahl, chairman of the Pryor School Board, says, "We realized early on that we wanted this for all our students. We believe that all children possess leadership abilities, and it is our job to help each child reach their fullest potential. Our sincere intent from the beginning, and our experience over the past fifteen years, has been that our community will be positively impacted by providing our students with these important leadership skills. Today, we have reached a point where we would not know how to do school without implementing the *Leader in Me* best practices." Today, all schools in the district—from the early learning center to elementary, middle, and high school—are actively participating, and according to Assistant Superintendent Dr. Tiffany Ballard, "*Leader in Me* is here to stay."

On a larger district scale, a visit to A.B. Combs Elementary inspired businessman Blake Sullivan to bring *Leader in Me* to the Bibb County School

District in Georgia. Sullivan's visit sparked a partnership with OneMacon (a collaborative of more than forty local organizations), the Macon-Bibb Chamber of Commerce, and the Bibb County School District. Together, they launched a bold initiative to embed leadership principles into every classroom in the district.

For the past decade, Bibb County School District has implemented the *Leader in Me* process districtwide. It started with a two-school pilot and expanded to all thirty-three schools and twenty-one thousand students within six years. The initiative has seen a 64 percent drop in behavior referrals, a 61 percent decrease in in-school suspensions, and graduation rates that went from 72 percent at the onset to the most recent 87 percent, an all-time high.

Bibb County superintendent Dr. Dan A. Sims credits the growth in graduation rates in part to *Leader in Me*'s focus on student agency, leadership, and readiness for life after high school. "It's not just about academic performance," says Dr. Sims. "It's about creating students who are more confident, more capable, and more connected to their purpose. *Leader in Me* provides students with a framework for life. It teaches them how to lead, how to listen, how to work with others, and how to take responsibility for their future. We are seeing the results not only in test scores, but in how students carry themselves every day. We are graduating not just scholars, but future-ready leaders with vision and character."

Several principals across the district, such as Latricia Reeves at Sonny Carter Elementary, indicated that they have witnessed dramatic shifts in school culture. "I have seen it transform our school," she says. Similar success is happening at Northeast High School, which became the first high school in the district and state to achieve Lighthouse Certification. As a bonus, Dr. Curtis Jones, who led much of the implementation, was named National Superintendent of the Year by the School Superintendents Association.

Other districts across the state have taken notice. In fact, more than one in five districts across Georgia are implementing *Leader in Me* to varying degrees. At a recent event at Vineville Academy, former state senate president pro tempore John F. Kennedy called *Leader in Me* "a model for what education can be," stating, "*Leader in Me* instills the type of principles we all want to see in our children—integrity, responsibility, teamwork, and purpose. This is not just a school program; it's a foundational change in how we prepare our young people for life. . . . With more than 265 schools now implementing this model, we are building a generation of students equipped not just for academic tests, but for life's greatest challenges."

A common thread in district implementations is the desire to give students the workforce readiness skills that are being requested by local businesses and, in some cases, mandated by their state. For example, District Superintendent Dr. Aaron Allen of Lincoln County Schools indicates, "In North Carolina, we have a portrait of a graduate that defines the ideal graduates coming out of our schools. It includes skills and traits such as personal responsibility, collaboration, critical thinking, adaptability, and empathy. It describes students who are able to make good decisions, who are proactive, and who think ahead and understand the importance of soft skills." Dr. Allen goes on to confirm, "Our *Leader in Me* journey has given us the vehicle to make that whole-school, whole-student experience happen from early childhood and all the way to graduation. It aligns well with the state portrait of a graduate."

The Northwest School District in Missouri became involved with *Leader in Me* partly because they wanted to improve the cultures and reputations of their schools. They started with three elementary schools, and now all seven of its schools are implementing it, along with its Early Childhood Learning Center, where three-to-four-year-olds are learning the *7 Habits*, running a student lighthouse team, setting goals, taking on leadership roles, and so forth. At the time the district began its *Leader in Me* journey, its high school was known as the "Prison on the Hill," mostly (but not entirely) due to its appearance on a hill. Students were reluctant to identify as part of the school. Today the high school has entirely flipped its reputation. Students want to attend that high school, particularly due to its students having such a large voice in what happens at the school. Visitors call on occasion to come see what they are doing. Six different student leadership teams have specific roles and meet regularly for a "meeting of the minds" to coordinate activities. The students let the adults know that their presence is optional at the meetings. They are organized. Furthermore, all the schools in the district benefit from schoolwide district activities that promote and sustain the culture of the entire district.

In short, districts of all sizes are implementing *Leader in Me*, from small single school districts to mammoth districts with dozens or even hundreds of schools. Districts hire *Leader in Me* for different reasons and to help solve different challenges. *Leader in Me*, in many ways, is like a Swiss Army knife and can be applied in myriad ways to solve lots of issues.

Many of the schools mentioned in previous chapters implemented *Leader in Me* as part of a district effort, as did several of the schools mentioned later in this chapter and beyond. These are only a few examples. Again, each district will implement the process in its own way to solve various challenges they are facing.

Community Engagements

A high percentage of *Leader in Me* schools enjoy some level of community or corporate sponsorship. Community and civic leaders know that good schools produce good workforces, and that good schools and good workforces attract outside businesses, investors, and home buyers. Strong students are a win for everyone.

In fact, we heard from a handful of community safety officers who view *Leader in Me* solely through the lens of what it will cost them if they don't provide life and workforce readiness skills for students. One county's juvenile rehabilitation administrator noted, "Save one student from being incarcerated and, on average, you will save the community six hundred thousand dollars in court fees, long-term prison costs, and rehabilitation expenses." For these and previously mentioned reasons, many community organizations are willing to sponsor schools in getting the skills offered through *Leader in Me*.

As with districts, we cannot begin to celebrate all the corporate and community organizations that have stepped up to support their local schools in pursuing *Leader in Me*. It would be an oversight not to honor at least a few of them, including organizations like the Chambers of Commerce, the United Way, and individual civic and business leaders.

The Chambers of Commerce. Our good friend the late Donnie Lane was a highly successful business leader in Alabama. When he learned what A.B. Combs was doing with the *7 Habits*, he piloted his own plane to take a few educators to visit the school. The *7 Habits* had greatly impacted his life and the way he led his company, so he couldn't help but wonder, "What might this do for students?" The group returned excited, and the local Chamber of Commerce agreed to fund a few schools to get started. The success of those schools spread to other schools around the state, and today *Leader in Me* schools are scattered throughout Alabama.

In fact, things went so well that Donnie and his Chamber partner, John Seymour, arranged for Dr. Covey to speak about *Leader in Me* at an American Chamber of Commerce Executives national convention. Nearly a thousand Chamber executives were in attendance. Several of those executives returned to their local Chambers and committed resources to bring *Leader in Me* to their community.

The largest Chamber initiative to first get underway was in Bowling Green, Kentucky, under the leadership of CEO Ron Bunch. Mr. Bunch says, "We got involved because our businesses said the present workforce lacked basic social and life skills. We see it as strategic for economic development, talent innovation, and matching people with jobs." After visiting one of their schools, a local businessman said, "I could interview three hundred adults for a line position at my factory and not one of them would shake my hand and look me in the eye like the young student who greeted me at the door tonight. If that's what this process does for kids, I'm in."

The Bowling Green initiative involved districts from ten counties, as well as mayors, university administrators, and several businesses. It is truly a symbiotic relationship. Sandra Baker, who is responsible for all the Chamber's education and workforce readiness initiatives, said, "Companies were voicing concerns that students were not coming prepared with the work-based readiness skills they needed to be successful in the workforce and saw *Leader in Me* as a long-game investment in the students and workforce of their county. We have been at it now for thirteen years. We see it as a 'boomerang effect.' If we provide great educational opportunities for our students and they have great memories of our community, we hope they will want to stay in our community and work, lead, serve, and raise families."

Superintendent Rob Clayton of Warren County Public Schools further explains, "We sat down with the local Chamber of Commerce to have a discussion about the needs from our business and industry partners. And through these discussions, we learned that there was a need for our students to be better equipped with the soft skills to ensure success in the workplace." That vision has been going on for more than a decade throughout the county, and is taking a new leap forward as construction is underway for what is being called an "IMPACT Center." It is a state-of-the-art secondary school built on the foundation of leadership development for all students and adults. Partnering with *Leader in Me*, the purpose-built facility serves as a model of what can happen when a district and school empowers students to lead, create, and drive change.

Another Chamber that soon got underway following the national convention was the Greater Cedar Valley Chamber, led by then CEO Bob Justis. Mr. Justis teamed with a local businessman, Tom Penaluna, CEO of the CBE Group, to start a pair of schools in two Cedar Valley districts. Tom even went so far as to have all 1,400 of his employees trained in the *7 Habits*. Things went well enough with those first two schools that the Chamber hired a former principal, Melissa Reade, to oversee the rollout of additional schools. Tom says, "It was the best decision we ever made." As more schools engaged, people started referring to Cedar Valley as Leader Valley. As of the last count, they have thirty-one schools in nine districts in the area implementing *Leader in Me*.

After seeing the success of Cedar Valley, more districts and more schools across Iowa have joined the journey. Tom concludes, "The work we do validates the impact that teaching students' leadership skills can have. *Leader in Me* is absolutely the right thing to do. We are making a difference for all students and are transforming the Cedar Valley region as a result. Our future looks bright because we are investing in our students now. I am so grateful to continue being part of this transformational process."

Another successful engagement from that first group of Chambers was started by Christi Kilroy at the Vicksburg–Warren County Chamber in Mississippi. She sums up the reality that many regions across the US face by saying, "*Leader in Me* fills in an enormous missing piece for us. The people funding the initiative in our area are the employers who are struggling to find people with basic skills, like getting to work on time. We can teach them technical skills, the business leaders say, but we cannot teach them how to get along with people, to get to work on time, or to have a plan. We wish students were getting these skills at home, but many are not."

The local Vicksburg–Warren County Chamber took their willingness to support *Leader in Me* to their area districts and schools to investigate their interest. A handful of schools showed immediate interest, so the Chamber started with them. A local car dealership volunteered to fund the initial roll-out. *Leader in Me* has since taken root in several districts and schools in the area at K–12 levels.

A few Chambers have partnered with districts to bring *Leader in Me* to their future workforces. Some Chamber leaders have taken the quest personally. One Chamber CEO got in front of an audience of educators who were exploring implementing *Leader in Me* in her area. She described how her third-grade son was diagnosed early on with dyslexia. With tears streaming down her cheeks, she told them how from day one teachers focused on his weaknesses. He was always perceived as a low test score. She said she would do anything to have her son in a school where people viewed him for his strengths, the boy who was highly energetic, a gifted artist, a singer, and filled with curiosity. She was willing to step up and raise funds for any school that would embark on a *Leader in Me* journey.

Chambers are wise not to push *Leader in Me* onto schools. They view it as a partnership, a choice.

The United Way. The efforts of local offices of the United Way have followed a similar path as those of the Chambers. The Quincy, Illinois, and Lafayette, Louisiana, locations are perfect examples.

Quincy is tucked between beautiful farm fields and the banks of the Mississippi River. The story there began with Dr. George Meyer, a former teacher, school administrator, and district superintendent. Upon retiring, he joined the staff at Quincy University, where he became dean of the School of Education. While there, he came across *The 7 Habits of Highly Effective People*. He became a certified *7 Habits* facilitator and began teaching the habits to education students. He then partnered with Principal Christie Dickens of Dewey Elementary to bring the habits to her school.

Things went well. Tardiness dropped 35 percent. The number of parents attending PTA meetings more than doubled. Disciplinary referrals dropped 75 percent, and referrals of students for completion of work declined 68 percent. Within two years the percentage of students passing end-of-grade reading tests jumped from 57.4 percent to 89.7 percent, and the percentage of students passing math jumped from 77.4 percent to 100 percent.

About the same time, the United Way of Adams County in Missouri was researching the best ways to contribute to its community. After reviewing several proposals and visiting *Leader in Me* schools, the United Way of Adams County was determined to take the *7 Habits* to all ten thousand students in their county. One of its leaders, Peggy Crim, noted that one of the things that drew their United Way to *Leader in Me* was that "it is not just for gifted students, or students with special needs, it is for all students." Six years into their efforts, eighteen schools and more than eight thousand students in the county were introduced to the *7 Habits*.

In Lafayette, Louisiana, Sarah Berthelot is chief operating officer for the United Way of Acadiana, which covers four parishes. She says their mission is focused on three pillars: education, raising income, and health care, and *Leader in Me* matches perfectly with their education pillar. They started by sponsoring one school, Martin Petitjean Elementary, which quickly began to see transformational changes. Attendance was up. Academics were up. But what Sarah and others saw as "even more noticeable were the intangibles, like the atmosphere between faculty, parents, and students." So they combined efforts with local civic leaders, the Chamber of Commerce, local businesses, the districts themselves, and the I Am a Leader Foundation to fund eight additional schools. Dr. Jason

Huffman, director of Impact Strategies for the United Way, has taken the lead on the effort and played a role in getting the various schools together once every five weeks to share best practices at the United Way offices. Martin Petitjean has become one of the featured Legacy Schools for *Leader in Me.*

Other civic-minded organizations, such as Rotary Clubs, Lions Clubs, and Kiwanis Clubs, as well as individual local businesses, have added their support through financial or nonfinancial means. We have singled these out as examples only because they were some of the first to get *Leader in Me* launched across national and even international boundaries. We are grateful for the contributions they have made to students in their communities and around the world.

Other Civic and Business Leaders. In several cases, it is not organizations that jump in and help, it is local individuals. Take Al Douglas and Glen Bressner, for example. They are influential members of the Lehigh Valley in Pennsylvania, visionaries, and big fans of the *7 Habits*. The two play golf together and discuss ways to enhance the Lehigh Valley region. They have sponsored several *Leader in Me* schools and recruited others from their pool of friends to sponsor additional schools.

Al Douglas describes his perspective on *Leader in Me* this way: "If I see something that I believe in, I try to go and make it happen. I have spent my entire career analyzing what makes great companies succeed. I was given a copy of *The Leader in Me* book and was convinced that it is needed in our schools. We need great school cultures where students are given opportunities to lead and serve and to understand the importance of making a difference. I shared the story with leaders in the Lehigh Valley, and we went about raising the money to make it happen. The Bethlehem School District in Pennsylvania is one of the fine examples of what happens when community leaders and schools work together to make a difference for their children."

Often, when we visit a school, we are welcomed by the community's mayor or other local civic leaders. Many of them have helped find grants or led fundraising efforts to bring *Leader in Me* to their schools. We love meeting them. Not all the support they offer is financial. Instead, they offer time to talk with students about careers and what it means to be a leader. Fire chiefs, police chiefs, doctors, scientists, authors, popular athletes, or other experts in their fields have much to offer besides food, prizes, entertainment, and money.

Many philanthropists reside outside the United States. Panamanian business leader Jose "Pepe" Miralles is one. As soon as he became familiar with *Leader in Me*, he knew it was something that his entire country needed.

Pepe knew that moving with that level of breadth at any kind of speed would require the support of the education ministry. As he met with the minister of education, he shared the vision of how *Leader in Me* could help transform in the country. What he didn't do was to ask for funding. All Pepe needed was for the minister to help open doors to speak with schools.

With the minister's support, Pepe and his wife, Paola, began visiting schools and listening to teachers and principals. They heard their worries, their dreams, and their willingness to work toward a new and better model of education. When they found teachers and schools that shared their vision, they then went to the local business leaders. They said, in essence, "This is your community, these are your schools, these students are your children and your future. We need your help." They made the offer so clear and reasonable that it was difficult for community and business leaders to turn it down.

One of the 155 schools and communities they are now working with is high in the mountains and has a majority of families with little money, little education, and a history of having had no voice as a people. Now these families are seeing profound transformation in their children and in their schools, and they are feeling a great impact in their communities. More than thirty thousand students, two thousand teachers, and twenty-seven thousand families have been impacted. Pepe says they are just getting started.

Foundations

A number of charitable foundations are likewise generous in lending support to schools. Among the early examples was the Panda Cares Foundation, founded by Peggy and Andrew Cherng, cofounders of the Panda Express restaurants. We mentioned them in Chapter 3.

You might recall that the Cherngs were impressed with A.B. Combs and the students' understanding of the *7 Habits*. About her first visit, Peggy remarked: "When we recruit leaders for our organization, we like people who are able to project their passion, who have self-confidence, and who have the right attitude to face the unknowns and the uncertainties that we all face every day in our personal or career lives. I saw all those traits in the children at A.B. Combs."

Following their visits, the Cherngs generously sponsored six schools near their corporate headquarters in Rosemead, California. Panda employees went the extra mile by organizing service projects to benefit the schools, including painting work. Before long, they expanded beyond their local community to sponsor an additional thirty schools in the western United States. That then evolved to more than eight hundred schools across the US, touching the lives of over four hundred thousand students.

The Cherngs set the pace for other foundations, such as the John Deere Foundation, headquartered in the Quad Cities area that borders Iowa and Illinois. It saw *Leader in Me* as compatible with its mission and as a way of giving back to its loyal customers and farming communities.

Robert and Patricia Kern were successful entrepreneurs who built a company in the Midwest that manufactured power generation equipment. They wanted to give back to their communities, so they set up the Kern Family Foundation. For years, their foundation has promoted human flourishing by supporting organizations and networks of organizations that build character in the next generation and that build the entrepreneurial spirit—the same things that helped make Robert and Patricia successful themselves.

FranklinCovey Education and the Kern Family Foundation began discussing their aligned missions and eventually formed a formal partnership. The Kern Family Foundation believed that if more schools could adopt *Leader in Me*, it would accelerate the character development of children and youth across the United States because of the principles *Leader in Me* teaches and the culture it creates within schools. Thus, the Kern Family Foundation began to help schools in financial need by subsidizing the cost of training and coaching for schools implementing *Leader in Me*. The Kern Family Foundation has now supported over a thousand schools across the US, and its impact will soon grow to many more schools, fulfilling their mission to build character in the rising generation.

Together, these foundations, community organizations, and individuals have contributed greatly to the rippling spread of *Leader in Me* schools across the globe.

Global Connect

One of our favorite community efforts is that of the *Leader in Me* Global Online Community. Via the *Leader in Me* website, schools around the world connect with each other and unite to engage in service learning projects or share cultural lessons with one another.

Consider a few examples:

US/Tanzania. When fourth-grade teacher Katie Chirhart from Shreve Island Elementary in Louisiana requested to connect with another class, Sylvia Ndekana, a teacher from Tanganyika International School in Tanzania, soon responded. Shortly thereafter, a group of students from each school got on a video call to get acquainted. When the Tanzanian students shared some words in Swahili, the students from Shreve Island were thrilled to hear a new language. "All of a sudden," said Katie, "they wanted to learn some more Swahili. They began thinking about how they could learn a second language. I could have taught them about the importance of learning a second language, but I doubt it would have mattered. Hearing it and experiencing it for themselves from new friends in a different country made all the difference." Sylvia says that her students now like to boast about having friends abroad. The two schools have since worked together on art projects, and they have undertaken a fundraising project to help an orphanage in Tanzania. "One of the most hopeful outcomes," says Sylvia, "is that both groups of students have commented that they look different from each other, but they have discovered that they are so alike. Building connections, understanding, and appreciation like this is invaluable."

Pakistan Plus Ten Countries. Another example of making global connections comes from Pakistan. When Mamoona Ali, a teacher at Beaconhouse WTC Gujranwala, discovered Global Connect, she immediately requested connections, which, over a period of six months, led to connections with fourteen schools in ten countries.

One of the connections came when the music teacher at the school created an original *7 Habits* song. Mamoona got the idea to invite students around the world to join the chorus. The first memorable music connection joined student voices from nine schools in singing the *7 Habits* song. "Music is universal, and the *7 Habits* connects us all," said Mamoona. Students from China, the US, Japan, the UK, Thailand, Malaysia, Brazil, and Indonesia participated in video rehearsals. Some recorded their singing part in Chinese, Malay, or Urdu, while others recorded in English.

Fourth-grade students from Richland Elementary in the US were among those who participated. Their teacher, Kathi Walker, commented: "Our students come from a small, rural community. Some have never been far from home and don't get the chance to experience cultures. Seeing them light up when they saw students in Pakistan, and then learning from their music teacher, was something neither I nor my students will ever forget. The experience was especially inspiring when the students made their best efforts to learn one of the lines of lyrics in Urdu, Pakistan's main language. I thought this would be too hard to do, but my students kept saying that they wanted to do it. It was exhilarating. My students got so excited. They brought books about Pakistan to class. We put up a map to see where we live and where Pakistan is."

Other connections Beaconhouse WTC Gujranwala has made include culture sharing, a pet show, sharing New Year's greetings, an Earth Day song, a favorite food day, kitchen gardening, recycling, sharing a favorite toy, *7 Habits* discussions, pen pals, and exchanges on helping special-needs students. Highlights included doing a virtual zoo visit and a project called Seeds of Hope, which got students planting trees on Earth Day.

England/US. In the United Kingdom, Queen Edith Primary School made pen pal connections with Jefferson Intermediate School in Missouri. Fourth graders wrote letters and mailed them to one another. Each student read their letter out loud to their class for a guided reading activity. "The children have been so inspired. They have been writing back straight away. Their handwriting and sentences are the best they have ever been, and there was no problem getting them to write," teacher Mel Lacey said. "They have previously had very little experience of letter writing and the joy it brings."

Banister Primary School in Southampton, also in England, likewise began their global connection as a pen pal exchange with third-grade classes at A.B. Combs. Teacher Alex Butler says that his students were more careful than ever with their writing because they knew their pen pal would be reading it. "I can't provide that kind of dynamic learning on my own," he says. Those positive connections led into conversations where students began to share their WIGs, data tracking, and progress. The students at each school became each other's accountability partners. They were thrilled and motivated to do this with new friends in another country.

Scotland/US/Pakistan. At Fair Isle Primary in Scotland, students had the idea to create a dance video with a great message: "We are going to light up the night." Teacher Claire Keith thought dancing with other schools around the world would bring more excitement and learning for her students. "For students, it's an especially fun and engaging activity," she said. Two schools in Pakistan and a US school in Buffalo, New York, joined in on the fun. Claire added, "This connection opened my students up to different countries in a personal way. They loved it and got a sense of appreciation for different cultures that I can't teach through books."

In Summary

Many schools could never implement *Leader in Me* without the sponsorship and support of corporate, community, and individual contributors, so not to recognize at least a portion of their generosity in this book would be a glaring omission. We acknowledge them for their contributions and reemphasize that they have more to contribute than funding as they share their life knowledge and their leadership knowledge and experiences.

Some educators fear that outside involvement will attract people who want to tell them how to run their school or get something in return. This has not been our experience. When Donnie Lane was asked what he expected in return for his contributions, he said that going into the schools and hearing the students speak the language of the *7 Habits*, seeing them set and achieve goals, and hearing parents speak about how their children apply the leadership principles at home was more than reward enough.

And so it is with most business leaders. It is a win-win for everyone.

Inspiring words remind students that character is as important as competence when being leaders.

8

Keeping It Alive

Leader in Me is a process, not a program or event. We refer to it as a slow cooker approach, not a microwave approach. It is not a quick fix.

Superintendent Dr. Aaron Allen of Lincoln County Schools recognizes that "if we are going to make lasting change, then we all know the research behind it. You've got to slowly bake it, slowly progress it, because not everybody is ready for it. We still have all these other mandates to worry about. So there's a balance to the rollout. The business community sees it and they want it now. But they, too, understand that progress of this nature takes time."

A.B. Combs has been implementing *Leader in Me* for more than twenty-five years. It didn't become what it is overnight. Each year it continues to make small tweaks and upgrades, but mostly it relies on its existing systems to keep it moving forward. Numerous other schools have also been implementing *Leader in Me* with fidelity for more than ten years. We call them Legacy Schools. After their initial launch, they, too, make adjustments and insert new ideas to keep things fresh and improving. Each is following its own path. Each is going at its own pace. No two are exactly alike.

For schools embarking on the *Leader in Me* journey, the best way we know to suggest how to successfully start and sustain *Leader in Me* over time is to apply *The 4 Essential Roles of Leadership*.[1]

The 4 Essential Roles of Leadership

The 4 Essential Roles of Leadership are used by top leaders and top organizations all over the world. They can be applied in organizations of all types—small and large. They can be applied in a school, a department, a grade-level team, a class, or a family. The *4 Roles* are: pathfinding, aligning, empowering, and, most importantly, modeling.

Pathfinding: Creating the Vision

The role of pathfinding is meant to give everyone involved a "big picture" vision of *Leader in Me*. A vision that says, "This is the path we want to go down to meet the needs of our stakeholders, including our staff, students, families, and community."

To create such a vision—or "path"—involves responding to three basic questions:

* Mission: What is our purpose in implementing *Leader in Me*?
* Strategy: How will we achieve the mission? How fast will we go?
* Goals: What are our most "wildly important" priorities?

Aligning: Executing Strategy

Leader in Me requires preparation, including the:

* Right Structures: Getting the right people in the right places.
* Right Systems: Creating systems to support and sustain the process.

Empowering: Coaching Potential

With clear vision and aligned structures and systems, effective leaders are set to empower teams and individuals to achieve the mission, vision, and strategy. As they do, they:

- Get to know people's strengths and interests.
- Offer people choice and voice; do not try to "control" them.
- Set clear win-win expectations and then "clear the path" of obstacles.
- Meet regularly to seek and provide feedback.
- Celebrate progress.

Modeling: Inspiring Trust

Highly effective leaders build trust by being trustworthy. They:

- Start by strengthening their character. Low character guarantees low trust.
- Develop their job-related competence.
- Live what they expect of others. Walk their talk.
- Consistently produce high-quality results.
- Lead from the inside out.

There is a logical sequence to *The 4 Essential Roles*. Pathfinding provides the path to which people and systems can be aligned. Aligning provides the systems and support to empower people. Empowering unleashes people's passions and energy to achieve the vision. Modeling and inspiring trust will always be at the center of everything effective leaders do because it impacts everything a leader does. It is an inside-out and ongoing process of continuous improvement.

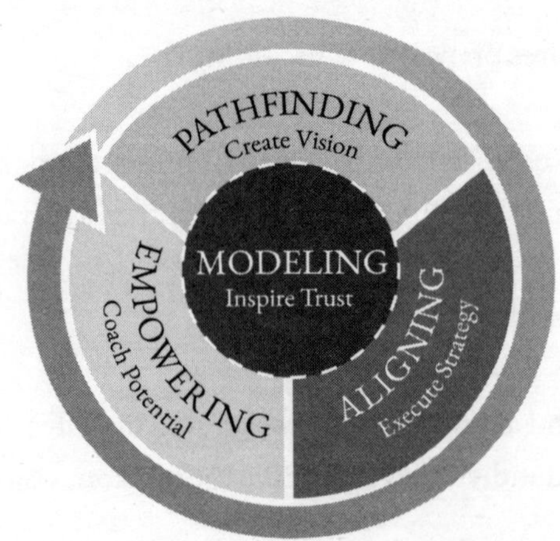

With that brief overview, let's explore what *Leader in Me* educators are doing to put *The 4 Essential Roles of Leadership* into action and get the result they desire.

Pathfinding: Creating Vision

"Transformation is everyone's job," observed quality guru Edwards Deming.[2]

If transformation is everyone's role in a school, then everyone deserves to have a basic understanding of what *Leader in Me* is before they commit to being a part of it. That begins with establishing a clear vision—or path—that will take a school from where it is to where it wants to go. That path includes a clear mission, strategy, and set of achievable goals.

Mission

Schools that embark on the *Leader in Me* journey put significant energy into earning people's commitment up front. That starts with an inspiring mission—a compelling *why*. Why do we exist as a school? What stakeholder needs are we trying to fill? To what will we say no?

Recall that when Muriel and her team set out to identify a new magnet theme for their school, they talked with the staff to get their input. They went to parents, community and business leaders, and even students to get their insights. They were assessing the desires of their stakeholders so they could identify a new magnet theme. Once they decided on leadership as their new theme, they came up with a new mission statement, which was: "To develop leaders, one child at a time."

Of course, nobody at that time fully knew what it was that they were committing to do. No school had ever done what they were about to do. They were the pioneers. It was a gradual process of trying new things, but they knew the purpose and the general outcomes they wanted to achieve.

Dr. Beth Sharpe at English Estates Elementary in Florida was one of the first principals to visit A.B. Combs to see what was happening. She was impressed and left determined to bring the process to her school. But first she needed to communicate to her staff what she had seen and to begin enlisting their commitment. There was still no formal process in place at that time to replicate what A.B. Combs had done, but Beth's team trusted her enough that they began discussing what their *Leader in Me* journey might entail.

And so it is for all school staffs. Each must determine their own mission—their own whys—for implementing *Leader in Me*. It's beginning with the end in mind.

An important principle to remember is "No involvement, no commitment." One principal shared how she read *The Leader in Me* and was excited to get started. Yet a handful of seasoned teachers were adamant about not doing it. The principal invited the teacher who was most resistant to visit a Leadership Day at A.B. Combs, since it was within driving distance. The teacher agreed. When she returned, she was still adamant, only this time she was adamant that they were going to do it. She declared to the other resisters: "There is no way we are not going to do this!" The school has now been implementing *Leader in Me* for more than ten years.

Another principal also had early resisters. Rather than push them into committing to participate, she chose to let those who did want to do it begin the process. Once the resisters saw what was happening in the classrooms of the early adopters, they wanted to join the process. That school, too, has now been implementing *Leader in Me* for more than ten years.

Once a school has committed to embarking on the *Leader in Me* journey, it is important to communicate its purposes and commitment to its stakeholders. One way to do that is to create a school mission statement and to share it widely. Principal Cris Edwards says that when her school created its school mission statement, students took a major lead in crafting it. A draft was then sent out to parents and community leaders for their input. In the end, they came up with: "To develop respectful, responsible learners and leaders." It now appears on school walls, in newsletters to parents, and in all communications to community leaders. It is a unifying reminder of the purposes the school is pursuing.

As weeks and years pass, a big part of keeping the mission statement fresh and alive is storytelling. A.B. Combs has a collection of stories that have been told and retold, again and again, to remind students and adults of their mission. For example, one day their music director, Jacquie Wojtowicz, was delayed in getting to her classroom. She arrived late to find a fourth grader standing in front of the choir directing warm-ups. She had been given no direction to do it. "Someone needed to step up and be the leader," said the young student. "So I did it." That story has been told and retold to give students a vision of what leadership looks like in a classroom and as a reminder of the school's mission.

One school dedicates an entire wall to telling and retelling stories. It is a long wall that students pass by every day, and it displays a giant timeline of inspiring stories that have taken place at the school. On it are numerous photos and accomplishments involving current and past teachers and students. Each photo or achievement reinforces the school's mission statement, which is: "We are a school where everyone is a leader."

As pleased as people can be with their school mission statement, teachers and students often get more excited about their class mission statements. That is because a common activity at the beginning of the year is for a class or advisory group to create a mission statement as a team. Students work together and get everyone's input on what to include in their class mission statement. Then a few students work together to polish it into a fine statement. Once it is done, all students feel a sense of ownership of it.

Taking things one step further, teachers and students write personal mission statements. Teachers will often post them outside their room or near their desk, while students typically place them in their leadership portfolios.

Of course, mission statements are not meant to just be hung on a wall or filed in a drawer. They are meant to be lived. They are meant to keep everyone's eyes on the whys.

Strategy

Strategy is the *how*: How are we going to achieve our purposes? How will we meet our stakeholders' needs this year? How fast will we go? Strategies are what turn a mission statement into doable, meaningful steps.

Research suggests that it takes three years to build a lasting, highly effective culture. So, even though *Leader in Me* schools will typically see noticeable impacts within the first three weeks, it is wise to create a strategy—or implementation plan—for pursuing a three-year path. In other words, think of *Leader in Me* as having multiple milestones, and consider taking them one year at a time. Have a year-one strategy, a year-two strategy, and so forth. It will provide order, make things feel manageable, save time in the long run, and increase the likelihood of success.

Depending on what other initiatives the school is already involved with, it may help to take a "go slow to go fast" approach. When Janson Elementary was approached by its district to explore its interest in adopting *Leader in Me*, the principal at the time, Dr. Gabriel Cardenas, wondered how his staff would respond to the idea. They were already stressed by large class sizes, low budgets, and other district initiatives. Nevertheless, enough teachers wanted to give it a try that they decided to get started, but to move slowly. The first year, the only thing they did was to learn about the *7 Habits* and start teaching the habits to students. Things went well that first year, and the teachers expressed a desire to move forward at a quicker pace. Now, more than ten years later, they, too, are a Legacy School.

Another best strategic practice is to build a yearlong timeline at the beginning of each new school year. In other words, plan out a *Leader in Me* calendar for the entire year. When will we have a Leadership Day? When will we hold student-led conferences? Will we have one or two *Leader in Me* parent nights? When will we teach the lessons? When will we have regular WIG sessions? When will we have celebrations? And so forth. Putting these events and goals on a timeline before the school year begins is a proactive approach that helps keep first things first and ensure that WIGs do not get swallowed up by PIGs.

Seeing the strategic plan drawn out in a timeline format gives staff a chance to give feedback: "That's too much." Or "Okay, that is reasonable." Or "This is the portion I can do." As the year progresses, the lighthouse teams or action teams can add to, subtract from, or adapt the timeline according to people's readiness to move forward.

Wildly Important Goals

When we asked the Legacy Schools' principals for advice for first-year principals, each independently gave the same reply: "Don't try to do too much. Decide your two or three highest priorities for year one, and then focus on implementing those first." Establishing a set of schoolwide Wildly Important Goals (WIGs) is one way to ensure this happens.

One district tasked a few schools with implementing *Leader in Me* as a way of improving attendance and enhancing their physical environments. The schools turned those tasks into a set of first-year WIGs. One WIG focused on attendance, and a second WIG focused on beautifying the hallways. They also used all *7 Habits* to talk with students about being at school on time. "What is the proactive way to get ready for school versus the reactive way?" Or "How do we put first things first when getting ready for school?" They did the same for the physical surroundings: "How can we synergize to make our school more beautiful?" They established clear lead and lag measures, made scoreboards for tracking progress, and held schoolwide meetings to discuss how they were doing.

While each school's reason for implementing *Leader in Me* will differ, each school can examine its mission and strategy to determine what its top WIGs will be for the year (or a shorter time period) and use the *4 Disciplines* to pursue its mission and strategy.

In short, by identifying which stakeholder needs it will meet (its mission), by planning how it will achieve its mission (its strategy), and by setting clear priorities (its WIGs), a school creates a clear vision and a path for how it will implement *Leader in Me*. It may adjust that path at times, and that is okay. But at least people will have a firm understanding from the start as to why the school is committing to *Leader in Me* and how it intends to achieve its mission.

Aligning

Prior to choosing "leadership" as its magnet theme, Muriel described A.B. Combs as a scattered mass of arrows. Everyone was going in their own direction and doing their own things. Though they were good things, none were aligned with any common school mission or path.

As with the vertebrae in a person's back or the wheels on a car, anytime there is a lack of alignment in a school, there is pain. Sometimes a lot of pain. For A.B. Combs, once it identified its mission, strategies, and goals, some of its pains began to be relieved. Part of the relief came from being able to say no to projects or requests that were not aligned with their new mission. Yet more pains remained.

The pains that remained were mostly a matter of getting people organized—who will do what?—and adjusting their existing systems to be more aligned with the new mission and strategy. In other words, A.B. Combs needed to make adjustments to align its organizational structure and systems with the new mission.

Aligning the Structure

Perhaps you have been part of a team like the following.

There were five talented people on the adult lighthouse team. Their names were Everybody, Anybody, Somebody, Nobody, and Busybody. One year there was a Wildly Important Goal to pursue. Everybody was asked to take part in it. Yet Everybody felt strongly that Anybody had the right talents to do it and was certain that Somebody would volunteer. So Everybody started working on some Pretty Important Goals. In the end, Nobody wound up working on the Wildly Important Goal, and that gave Busybody plenty to complain about. If you have been part of such a misaligned team, then you know something about pain.

Aligning the structure is a matter of getting the right people into the right places and having clear roles and responsibilities. Schools or grade-level teams need to be organized (structured) and specific responsibilities divided up so that people know what is expected of them and when.

The best *Leader in Me* implementations always include the synergistic efforts of all staff and all students, and even some parents and community members. For starters, at the helm of every strong *Leader in Me* school is a strong principal. It is important that the principal is supportive of *Leader in Me* and is seen walking the talk. But the principal does not need to be in charge of everything or be involved in every decision. They can delegate responsibilities to others. In fact, schools are often encouraged to identify an assistant principal or school counselor to coordinate much of the responsibility for implementation. But even that individual is not meant to carry the efforts alone. This is where the lighthouse teams, which we described in Chapter 4, come into play.

Most *Leader in Me* schools have two lighthouse teams, one for adults and one for students. The lighthouse teams' main responsibilities are to oversee the implementation of *Leader in Me*. They are made up of individuals who represent the varying perspectives and needs of the school. For example, the adult lighthouse team might consist of seven to ten members, such as the principal, an assistant principal, a school counselor, a few teachers who represent various grade levels or departments, and perhaps a parent or two. The student lighthouse team might consist of anywhere from ten to twenty students who represent various grade levels and backgrounds of the student population. They are not the same students who are always chosen to be leaders, but are students who have a variety of talents and can influence a broad range of students. A few students may be included simply because they need an extra boost of self-worth.

Early on, the lighthouse teams may consist of temporary members who are handpicked to get things launched. But over time, the freshness of the lighthouse team is kept alive by rotating in a few new members who have new ideas and perspectives on an annual or as-needed basis.

The lighthouse teams are also not intended to do all the planning and work. Instead, one of their main roles is to be in charge of spreading out the work so that anyone who wants to contribute can. After all, remember the paradigms "everyone has genius" and "everyone can be a leader." One way that happens is for the lighthouse teams to create action teams. For example, we have seen some student lighthouse teams that have as many as eighty students. Basically, any student who wants to be on the student lighthouse team can be on it. But in that case, there are still only ten to twenty students who are on the main team, and the other students are part of action teams. Action teams are given specific assignments. For example, there might be action teams that conduct morning announcements, plan a specific assembly, lead an annual activity, or organize a service learning project. Their responsibility may last only as long as that one responsibility, but they lead it, plan it, recruit participants, advertise it, and guide it to completion.

The adult lighthouse team's main responsibility is twofold. One, let the students lead as much as possible while playing the role of mentors and guides on the side. They do their best to ensure that the students succeed in a way that allows them to say "We did it all ourselves." Two, ensure that the adults in the school are well cared for. Remember the adults.

Lighthouse teams meet on a regular basis. They are considerate of people's availabilities and bandwidth. For example, some student lighthouse teams avoid meeting before or after school out of consideration for students who are limited by bus schedules or extracurriculars. Many secondary schools assign the student lighthouse team to the same advisory period so they can meet together regularly. At secondary schools, the ideal is for the student lighthouse team to be part of a designated class so the students have sufficient in-school time to meet and plan together.

In the end, the ideal is to have everyone contributing and everyone feeling ownership for the good of the school.

Aligning the Systems

With a clear path and an organized structure of who will do what, an important next step is to align some of the school's existing systems with the path.

Systems are meant to make things easier for teachers. They sustain progress over time. They make it so that teachers do not need to reinvent the wheel each year. In the words of Dr. Kim Cummins, principal of Martin Petitjean Elementary, "*Leader in Me* is at the epicenter of everything we do, and systems are what keep it going and alive. If I were to leave, everything would keep going because there are systems in place."

Any school that has been doing *Leader in Me* successfully over time can show you the systems they have tailored to fit their needs and talents. There are systems for tracking progress on WIGs, creating lesson plans, writing classroom mission statements, establishing agendas for class meetings, and so forth. Indeed, there are systems for carrying out most parts of *Leader in Me*. Many are available through the *Leader in Me* website.

At the school level, a few systems are common that play a large role in sustaining *Leader in Me*. They include:

* Development Systems
* Communication Systems
* Selection Systems
* Collaboration Systems
* Feedback Systems
* Celebration Systems

Development Systems. Often called learning systems, development systems inform both new and existing adults and students about *Leader in Me*. In addition to the initial training adults and students receive at the start of implementing *Leader in Me*, they might include:

* *Training for New Students.* Imagine the surprise new students might have when arriving at a new school. "What is this language everyone is speaking?" "What do you mean by lighthouse team?" "What is a WIG?" To prepare such students, schools provide an opportunity—such as a two-hour introductory overview for new students—to acquaint them with the *7 Habits* and explain why students seem to be leading the school instead of adults.
* *Training for New Staff.* As soon as convenient (preferably before a new school year), newly hired staff—teachers and nonteaching staff—receive training in the *7 Habits* and an overview of *Leader in Me*. Principals find it valuable to participate in these overviews so that newcomers know of their personal commitment to *Leader in Me*.

It is not uncommon for such overviews to be facilitated by multiple teachers. That way, new staff not only learn the content but also begin building relationships with existing staff.

- *Ongoing Boosters.* Ongoing boosters are provided to staff periodically throughout the year to deepen their understanding of the *7 Habits* and *Leader in Me* best practices. Once again, many boosters are supported by a library of resources and videos on the *Leader in Me* website.
- *Mentoring.* Several schools assign *Leader in Me* mentors for new teachers. They are available to answer any questions a new teacher might have. Several schools also mentor other schools in their district. In the process of mentoring the other schools, they deepen their own understanding of *Leader in Me*.

In addition to their internal development systems, many schools take advantage of FranklinCovey development systems, such as:

- *Leader in Me Weekly.* FranklinCovey implementation resources and videos to share best practices from the *Leader in Me* global community.
- *Symposium.* Multiple times a year, FranklinCovey Education hosts regional symposia where guest keynote speakers present, schools lead breakout sessions, visits to schools are made, and preconference workshops are provided.
- *Coaching.* Certified coaches are available to work with schools and small teams, as well as provide professional executive coaching for principals and district-level leaders.

These are just some of the systems and opportunities where students and adults—both new and ongoing—are given opportunities to learn and refresh their knowledge of *Leader in Me* and its main components.

Communication Systems. All schools have systems for communicating with students, parents, and staff. Common systems include morning announcements, newsletters, assemblies, take-home packets, parent nights, phone calls, emails, apps, parent-teacher conferences, bulletin boards, social media blogs, and websites. The language of leadership can be embedded into all of them.

One school uses their phone answering system to communicate how it values students. When calling after-hours, a prerecorded student voice answers, "Hi, this is [name]. I am a leader at [name] Elementary. It is now after-hours. Please call back between 8:00 a.m. and 4:00 p.m., and make it a great day." The system communicates more than the school's hours. It communicates that students at the school can be trusted with adult responsibilities. Students live for the chance to be "voice of the week," and they work hard to practice their diction and public speaking skills so they can do it right.

Many, if not most, of these communication systems are already in place in schools. They just need to be slightly adjusted to align with the leadership theme.

Collaboration Systems. It is not enough to tell staff, "Everyone find time to talk and share." Systems must be put in place for collaboration to happen on a consistent basis. Many schools, for example, participate in professional learning communities. These can be used as opportunities for teachers to connect and collaborate around *Leader in Me* best practices.

A.B. Combs has a daily collaboration system called "hallway huddles." Prior to school starting each morning, music (selected by teachers) sounds over the intercom to let teachers know it is time to gather in the hall outside their classrooms. They spend ten minutes conversing and collaborating about important things they are working on that day. It is a chance to discuss students who need special attention, coordinate activities and schedules, and address concerns. It lasts only minutes but is a built-in system that ensures collaboration.

A collaboration system that some *Leader in Me* schools have established is an annual staff field trip. Where do they go on this big field trip? They travel from classroom to classroom and office to office within the school. They observe what other teachers and staff members are doing with lesson plans, bulletin boards, counseling sessions, and so forth. It is a potpourri of ideas and a way for teachers to be acknowledged. No bus is needed. Another school calls this "going fishing." A couple of times each year they "go fishing" in each other's classrooms to catch new ideas and applaud creativity.

Selection Systems. Highly effective organizations are made up of highly effective people. So for schools to launch and sustain *Leader in Me* in an effective way requires hiring and retaining the right people.

One principal shared: "To select new teachers for our school, we pick people who pick us. We make sure they are wanting to be with us on our *Leader in Me* path, because we do expect a little more than other schools."

We fully understand that not all pools of potential teaching candidates are equal. Some schools have better choices than others. But that is why some schools go to great efforts to be at the hiring forefront. They start by making their schools the best schools. The best schools tend to attract the best teachers. Principal Melody Hazeltine of Neil Armstrong Elementary, a Legacy School in Florida, was pleased to tell us: "We have teachers start reaching out to us starting in January, asking us to consider them for hire. They know we are a *Leader in Me* school, they've heard what we are doing, and they want to be a part of it. Our reputation is our best way of improving our future pool of teachers."

As another principal put it, "We look for teachers who truly care about students. We can coach new teachers on how to teach. What is hard is to teach people how to care." That is why some principals give teacher candidates a copy of *The Leader in Me* and ask them to read it prior to their interview. If they return without at least some sparkle in their eyes, that is all the principal needs to know in answer to the question of whether to hire the candidate.

When it comes to hiring the best teachers, nothing compares to rerecruiting and rehiring the best teachers the school already has. In fact, one of the best results schools report with *Leader in Me* is that they experience lower teacher turnover. Granted, some teachers will say "This is not for me" and leave, but, by and large, turnover is lower at *Leader in Me* schools.

Recruiting all people—not just teachers—with *7 Habits* qualities is not always easy, but it is easier than hiring people with the opposite qualities and then dealing with the negative consequences. That is why it is important to consider ways to integrate *Leader in Me* into a school's hiring systems. And that is especially the case when hiring a new principal.

Everyone at A.B. Combs knew the day would eventually come, though no one liked to think about it. But the day did eventually come for Muriel to retire as principal. Who could replace her? The school district wanted to be thorough and fair in selecting a replacement. As part of its due diligence, the district interviewed several A.B. Combs teachers to determine what key attributes were needed for the new principal. The teachers were not allowed to name names of who they thought the new principal should be, so the teachers were careful not to mention any particular candidate. But one teacher confessed that she did identify a few specific attributes, like "She needs to do her eye makeup beautifully to go with her beautiful eyes." It was her way of being clear: "We want Juley!"

The district was fair and thorough in its search for a new principal, and, yes, it did select Juley Sexton as the new principal. She had been in the role of assistant principal for several years. There was seldom something important that Muriel was a part of that Juley was not a part of. Juley knew the key stakeholders as well as anyone—the teachers, parents, students, district, and community. She had been involved with *Leader in Me* from its beginnings. She had the staff's full support. Today the staff may laugh and joke that Juley does have nice eyes and makeup, but what they will really be trying to communicate is that she is doing an outstanding job as Muriel's successor.

The quality of a principal can greatly influence the effectiveness of any school-level implementation process, including *Leader in Me*. The passion of the principal tends to trickle down to the staff. So having a succession plan is important.

While having a succession plan for the principal is important, the same is true for any key role. We were impressed when we met with the high school student lighthouse team at the Colegio Suizo Americano in Guatemala. The team was organized and student-led. As they went around the room one by one to tell us their specific roles, a number of students were pointed out as having specific roles for the next year's student lighthouse team. They were in training to take on those key roles the next year. They, too, had a succession system.

Feedback Systems. As the old saying goes: "What gets measured gets done."

At the end of year one, a school sent out its annual parent feedback survey. Eighty parents responded. That was up from thirty parents the year prior to *Leader in Me*. One hundred percent of the parents gave teaching the *7 Habits* a "very favorable" rating. It let the school know it was heading in a positive direction with the support of parents. That same school's student population was about to drop by fifty students due to the aging population in its boundaries. That meant it was about to lose two teaching positions. The principal worried, "Which two teachers will have to go?" But as the summer started, the principal got a knock at his door. It was a parent who lived outside the school's boundaries who had heard the school was doing *Leader in Me*. She wanted to enroll her children. Amazingly, that happened several times over the summer. Parents from outside the school's boundaries had heard what the school was doing and wanted to enroll their children. When the next school year arrived, the school was at full enrollment and no teachers were lost. That, too, is good feedback.

Much of the feedback that many schools receive about their performance is anecdotal—a story here and a story there. It is largely reactive. If it comes, it comes. They do not seek it out. *Leader in Me* schools prefer a proactive approach. It uses a Measurable Results Assessment (MRA) to collect feedback from all staff, students, and parents regarding how things are going. The schools use it to make adjustments and set WIGs for the following year. That is because the important thing about collecting feedback is to not just listen to it but to act on it as it relates to the school's mission.

Celebration Systems. Closely tied to evaluation systems are reward systems. They are intended to celebrate, motivate, and reinforce success.

Educators like to debate whether intrinsic rewards are better than extrinsic rewards. Intrinsic rewards always seem to win out in the research as being most motivating and reinforcing. Don't be surprised, however, if students thrive on the extrinsic rewards, such as prizes, treats, extra playtime, etc. Whenever extrinsic rewards are used, we suggest pairing them with intrinsic rewards: "Here is your treat. Have I ever told you how much I admire your work ethic and your attention to detail? I really admire you for that. So I hope you enjoy your treat."

Whether intrinsic or extrinsic, rewards do not need to be large to be effective. One teacher had an old pair of socks hanging from a hook near the front of the room. When we asked her about the socks, she laughed and said, "My students knocked my socks off today with their outstanding classroom manners, and I wanted to let them know it. The way I do it is to hang up the socks, and when they see them, they know we are going to leave early for recess, and they get all excited." It is not hard to imagine her students trotting off to recess with an extra skip in their step because they knew their teacher had caught them doing something good.

As Muriel relates, "You will hear effective teachers compliment students all the time. You will hear them thank them and tell them how much they appreciate them. You will hear them telling students they believe in them. If there are students being disruptive, you will hear their teacher reward the ones who are not with a thank-you. You will see them catch and reward students for doing something 'right' far more than you will ever see them catch and scold students for doing something 'wrong.' It is a positive way of connecting with them every day." Not all children receive those kinds of verbal rewards at home. And it helps when teachers build them into their daily systems.

When a school has the right people committed and serving in the right roles and supported by the right systems, that school is said to be in alignment with its mission and stakeholder needs. If it were to be illustrated as an image, it would look something like the illustration on the following page, as opposed to the misaligned arrows that Muriel used to describe her school prior to *Leader in Me*. Granted, in most cases, there will always be a few arrows that are misaligned—no school is perfect. But focus on involving people to gain their commitment, get the right structure in place, and align the arrows to achieve the mission, strategies, and WIGs, and stakeholders are nearly certain to be satisfied.

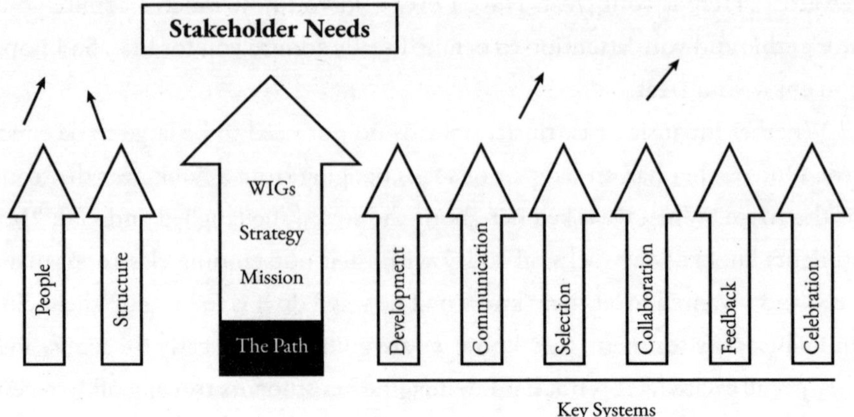

Empowering

As previously mentioned, when it comes to empowering people, a central definition of leadership with *Leader in Me* is: "Leadership is communicating people's worth and potential so clearly that they are inspired to see it in themselves." The goal of empowering students is not just to communicate students' worth and potential, but to nurture and grow it.

When Dr. Covey graduated from Harvard's MBA program, his brother, John, asked him what he wanted to do in life. Stephen responded with three words: "Release human potential." And that is what he always attempted to do as a teacher. He saw his students as having much potential and wanted to teach in a way that would bring out that potential.

Yet as he turned to speaking in front of large audiences of adults, Dr. Covey would often ask the audience, "How many of you feel you have more talents and more contributions that are not being used by your current organizations?" Nearly everyone would raise their hand. What would the response be in your school if all students were asked that same question? Would they feel their talents and contributions were being fully utilized? What about the staff? What would they say?

To launch and sustain *Leader in Me* requires that the five core paradigms become the central foundation of the school's culture. Everyone—students and adults—are viewed as having genius in them and being capable of being leaders. People need to work from a paradigm of "change starts with me."

And yet for some educators, it is a difficult shift to view themselves as a "guide on the side" rather than the "sage on the stage" and the one who is always in control versus the one who lets others lead out. It may be the hardest part of transitioning to a *Leader in Me* culture at some schools. It will be evident in the way they teach lessons, resolve discipline issues, or plan events. Do they "let go" of some aspects of their role and let students lead out, or feel the need to direct every decision in fear that a student may not do everything to perfection?

Dan McQueery is the principal at Fort Zumwalt Middle School. Some of his 1,200 students come from *Leader in Me* elementary feeder schools. Once they got to middle school, however, they saw little evidence of *Leader in Me*. So they approached Mr. McQueery and let him know they wanted more voice in the school. To his credit, Mr. McQueery responded that he was happy to give it a try.

Largely with the students' input, the first thing they did was establish a student lighthouse team. It was heavily led by some of the sixth graders who had been members of lighthouse teams at their elementary school. They were new to the school but not new to running a lighthouse team. Furthermore, a multimedia team was created, and it took over responsibilities for morning announcements. As part of their broadcasts, they focused on a habit a month as a theme. That required students to start making monthly videos to go with each of the *7 Habits*. The adults thought the videos were silly, but students thought they were awesome.

In addition to teaching the leadership principles to their peers, students were given opportunities to teach *7 Habits* "boosters" to the teachers during development days. The adults were totally entertained by the clever skits and activities the students designed just for them. Connections were being built between students and the adults.

Gradually, Mr. McQueery's approach went from "Let's see how this goes" to "I now try to stay out of their way." There are twenty-seven students on the student lighthouse team. They organized themselves with a president and multiple action teams led by students. Mr. McQueery asks them what they want to do, and then he does his best to be sure they are supported. The more the student lighthouse team flourished that first year, the more teachers could truly tell, "Students want this!" That led to more teachers wanting to join in on the excitement. Students feel empowered. With every success, they hear the message from the adults: "We believe in you."

One of the side benefits of empowering students that Mr. McQueery conveys is that he feels more connected with all the students. He says that prior to *Leader in Me* his days were devoted to working with students who were "in trouble," whereas now he is connecting and connected with most all of the students. He admits that "students can be difficult to connect with at times. But once you make the effort to connect with them, they are amazing."

One of the schools that A.B. Combs students feed into is Carroll Middle School. It is also a *Leader in Me* school. When students show up there, they fully expect to have their voices heard. After all, that is what they have been accustomed to their entire school lives.

Yet in the early stages, when some of those students arrived at the middle school, they were surprised to learn that there were some rules in place that felt controlling, not empowering. For one, students had restricted seating in the cafeteria, which kept them from sitting with some of their friends. They knew that the rule had been put in place as a result of past incidents, but they felt that if students could set the rules, then students would be more inclined to follow the rules. They wanted the chance to make new rules and give those new rules a chance. If the new rules didn't work, they would go back to the assigned seating.

Principal Tina Zarzecki loved the students' proactivity. She listened. She gave them the freedom to create the new rules. They synergized. They presented their new rules to the other students to get their commitment. A full year later, everyone agrees that things are better with the new rules. Students are mingling with each other in respectful ways. Students are happy. Adults are happy. All because students trusted their principal enough to approach her and express their voices and solutions, and because the principal entrusted them to make the new rules. They went from a feeling of being controlled to a feeling of being empowered—released. That one success resulted in further decisions being turned over to students and giving them more voice.

Again, for *Leader in Me* to take full root and be sustained over time, there need to be trust and empowerment with people's talents and contributions being released and given opportunities to be utilized.

Something we truly enjoy about teachers is that when we show them a best practice from another school—such as a new idea for a bulletin board or hallway display—they will inevitably praise it and say "Oooh!" and "Aaah!" Yet the entire time they are thinking in their minds, "I can do something better than that." And they do. They take the idea and then find ways to apply it using their own talents and creativity. And it comes out looking fantastic. They are proud of it and proud to be a teacher.

Indeed, one of the best ways to launch and sustain *Leader in Me* over time is exactly what we've emphasized since the opening chapter: Make your school one of a kind and empower teachers to make their classrooms one of a kind.

When one principal learned her entire school district planned to implement *Leader in Me*, she was nervous. Even a little upset. She viewed it as "one more thing." But after learning more about it, she asked, "Can I make it my own?" She was told that she not only could make it her own, but that she was fully expected to make it her own. She and her staff immediately went from being hesitant to being delighted. They have since created a fine *Leader in Me* school, and she and her team have definitely done it their way.

As Principal Matt Thornhill puts it, "*Leader in Me* gives us a framework, but there are lots of ways to get there. We love that it provides the autonomy for how we do what we do. Not every school will do it the same, and we like that."

Empowerment takes patience. Success does not happen all at once or overnight. Some teachers may find *Leader in Me* daunting at first. Take it a step at a time. Go at your own pace. One teacher shared how in the beginning she was worried she couldn't do it. But then in hindsight she looked back and declared, "It's super easy to do. I just find small ways to blend it into everything we're already doing." Another teacher wondered how it was going to work in the beginning, but she took it one step at a time and now says, "It doesn't really require a lot of change on my part in terms of how I do things. It has just become part of the language and routine that I use. It is at the center of what I do to encourage and support students."

Modeling

The last of the *4 Essential Roles* is actually the central core to all the other roles. "What the world needs most," according to Dr. Covey, "is fewer critics and more models."

There are two things that deserve to be modeled in a school for it to have a thriving culture and desirable results: character and competence.

If you are told by your doctor that you need heart surgery, who would you prefer: a doctor with high character or a doctor with high competence? Can you imagine choosing a doctor solely due to high character, knowing the doctor was not competent? The good news in that scenario is that the doctor would never perform the surgery unless it is necessary. Or what if you knew a doctor was competent and had a near–100 percent success rate on doing heart surgery but also that they had been accused of performing expensive heart surgeries that were unnecessary but profited them well? Would you be eager to choose that doctor?

Just as you would prefer a doctor to have both character and competence, students and parents prefer teachers and other adult staff to have high character and high competence. They want someone who is not just teaching the *7 Habits* well, but someone who is living the habits well. It is hard, if not impossible, to imagine being effective at pathfinding, aligning, or empowering if one does not have the competence or the character to lead out in those roles. Try empowering an adult or a student who sees you as lacking character or competence.

So, the place to start launching and sustaining *Leader in Me* over time is with oneself, and by working on modeling and remodeling the five core paradigms. For some educators, *Leader in Me* involves very little shift in paradigm. They have been thinking and doing things in harmony with the core paradigms their entire career. For others, some paradigms might represent sizeable shifts. So for *Leader in Me* to be sustained, some educators will need to consistently remind themselves and repeatedly work on the paradigms as adults, and they'll need to do so prior to expecting students or parents to apply them.

It is an inside-out process.

Excellence Is a Journey

When her school was designated a lighthouse school, Principal Ramona Dunn said, "The award is not a capstone, it's a milestone on our journey." Indeed, excellence is a journey, not a final destination. No change effort of any sizeable scale or value comes without bumps, gaffes, and bruises. So staff members must be prepared to learn, laugh, and lead again.

As Dr. John Shepard indicates, "Lighthouse teams need to be okay with failure in the beginning. They need to be okay with hearing criticism and people wanting to make it better. Do not expect things to go perfect on the first try."

Chances are you will implement some portions of *Leader in Me* and things will go well from the beginning. Other efforts might get off to a rough start. It may take time to tailor your efforts to match your specific situations and students. What works well one year may not work as well the next. It is a matter of continuous improvement.

Many factors go into determining the proper path and pace for school transformation. It is often a matter of finding the right balance between too little or too much.

Too Little	Too Much
No compelling purpose for change	Purpose not hitched to reality
People unwilling to change	People change too often, careen from fad to fad
Lack of a strong principal	Too dependent on a strong principal
Not enough time spent getting buy-in	Excessive time trying to gain total consensus
Lack of strategy	Strategy too detailed—people not empowered
Not enough preparation, planning	Always planning but never implementing
Move too slow—people lose enthusiasm	Move too fast—people feel overwhelmed
Not enough teamwork—individuals do their own thing	Too much team focus—individual effort stifled
Successes not recognized or rewarded	Successes declared too soon or overpraised
No accountability or feedback	Too much checking up—micromanaging
Not enough district support	District imposes the change
Give up too soon	Keep doing the same things when they don't work
Students are not involved	Students are overinvolved
Not enough doing	Lots of talking

Simplify, Simplify

Lastly, as Henry David Thoreau observed about living life, "Simplify, simplify."[3] So it is with launching and sustaining *Leader in Me*.

Once again, take *Leader in Me* a step at a time. "There are a lot of pieces to *Leader in Me*," says Assistant Principal Brianna Welsh when giving advice to a new *Leader in Me* school getting ready to start. "So we put them into digestible bites and focus on doing each bite well. We look at what our most important needs are at the moment, and we start there. Otherwise, it can be overwhelming."

Principal Jennifer Million agrees. "The main thing in the beginning is to keep the main things the main things," she says. "Identify and handle what is most important to the success of your school and don't lose focus."

In other words, "Simplify. Simplify."

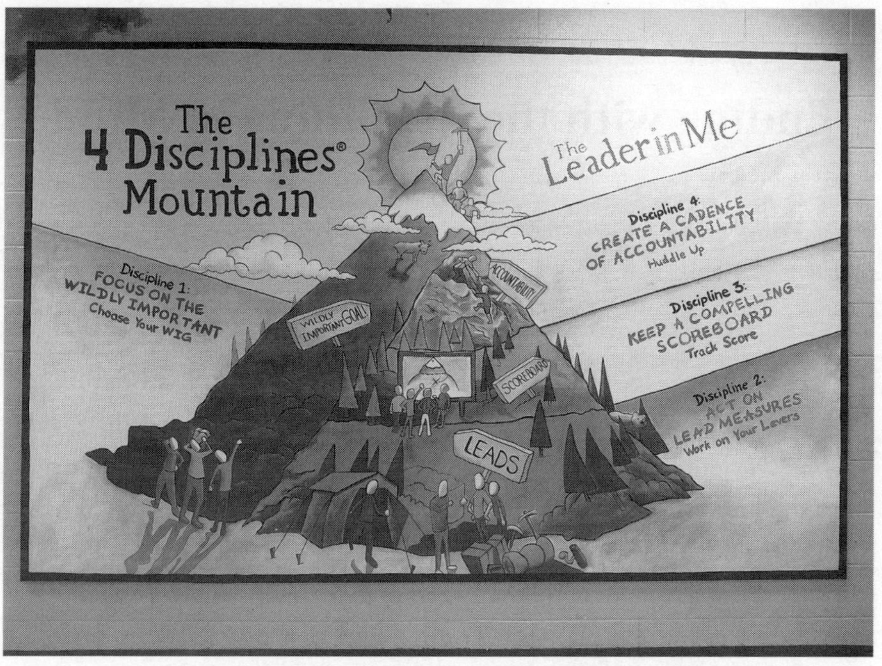

A large hallway mural illustrates "The 4 Disciplines Mountain," guiding students through the goal-setting process.

9

Ending with the Beginning in Mind

Shawn Maggiolo, fifth-grade teacher at A.B. Combs, has been one of the teachers to make the entire twenty-five-years-and-counting *Leader in Me* journey. She has witnessed *Leader in Me* from its earliest beginnings and knows firsthand what does and does not work. She has felt its many benefits. Yet not even Shawn anticipated what occurred when she was teaching students about timelines and how to create them. Each student was to draw a personal timeline and place on it eight events that they felt were the most important events of their young lives. She made no suggestions about what they should place on their timelines. When the timelines were finished, Shawn asked the students to identify the one event that they saw as being the most impactful. Half of the students had chosen attending A.B. Combs as their top life event.

Shawn asked the students *why*. Why did they choose A.B. Combs as their top life event? They said they loved the school environment. They loved being viewed as leaders. Some said it was the first time someone believed in them. They felt valued. Their expressions were deeply sincere. Shawn literally fought back tears. All her work had not been forgotten. It was worth the effort.

One of the students described how he had moved to A.B. Combs from another school. "My other school was all about reading, writing, and math.

Here it is about how you treat people, and what you want to do with your life." He carried on about the difference it had made for him. And that was the point when Shawn grabbed a tissue and faked a sneeze. Her emotions were tender. All her hard work and all her beliefs about how to work with children were being validated. She felt she had contributed a small part to what these children were telling her. She was making an important difference.

Not "One More Thing"

Leader in Me faces the same obstacle that any school transformation process of such a magnitude faces. How to make it feel like it is not "one more thing."

The last thing educators want to hear is that they must run faster. Most are already doing more than they have reasonable capacity for. And yet, what teacher, what parent, what future employer would not want students to learn how to:

Be Proactive. To take responsibility for their education and life. To take initiative and not to be emotionally reactive.

Begin with the End in Mind. To plan. To have a clear understanding of what is most meaningful and important to them. To set goals. To be forward-thinking.

Put First Things First. To know how to manage time wisely and focus on the highest priorities. To say no to unimportant activities or pressures. To become self-reliant, "independent."

Think Win-Win. To be considerate of others while having the courage to stand up for their own wants and rights.

Seek First to Understand, Then to Be Understood. To be both a good listener and able to communicate thoughts clearly.

Synergize. To work well with people of different backgrounds and optimize people's strengths. To produce creative team outcomes. To be "interdependent."

Sharpen the Saw. To continuously renew and improve their physical, emotional, and mental capacities. To keep their spirits high.

Find Their Voice and Inspire Others to Find Theirs. To discover, nurture, and share their own talents while helping others discover theirs.

All *7 Habits* and the other leadership principles they learn as part of *Leader in Me* are important for students of all ages. And so it thrills us when we visit with teachers who say, "This is not just one more thing, it is a better way of doing what we are already doing."

There are at least five reasons why teachers might feel this way:

#1: Leader in Me is an operating system, not another app. Leader in Me is a way of thinking, a set of core paradigms, an organizing system. It is not one more app to put on a computer or cell phone. It is the operating system itself. Teachers can run all kinds of programs on it. Once in place, it enables all the other apps, of which there are many, to run smoother and more efficiently. In fact, numerous schools that already have other programs or initiatives in place report that *Leader in Me* has helped them strengthen those initiatives.

#2: Leader in Me is an integrated, ubiquitous approach. Once the *7 Habits* and other leadership skills have been taught, they can be integrated into any existing subject matter topic or most any lesson plan that teachers are already teaching. Teachers just need to help students see and make the connections. And by teaching the leadership skills, teachers are either directly or indirectly influencing the culture and academics of a school. It is all integrated.

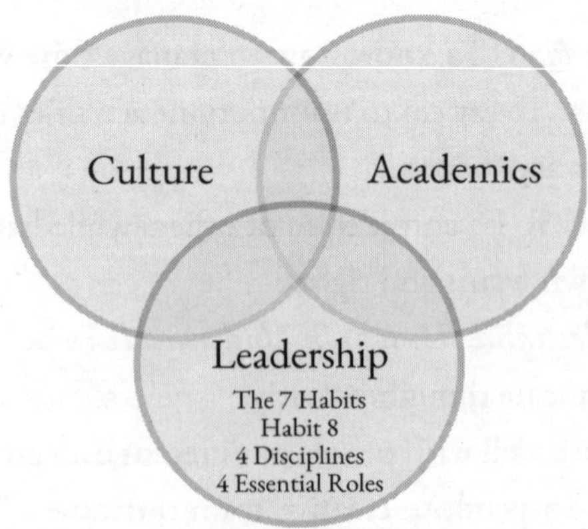

#3: Leader in Me helps educators focus on what is most important. By identifying Wildly Important Goals (WIGs), educators can focus on the highest

priorities and say no to tasks that do not sufficiently contribute to meeting stakeholders' needs. According to Richard DuFour and Robert Eaker:

> It is time to recognize that the major flaw in the de facto curriculum of American public schools is not that schools do not do enough, but that they attempt to do too much. Even though American students have fewer school days each year than their Asian and European counterparts, they are expected to learn far more curriculum content. Confronted with a curriculum that is "a mile long and one-half inch deep," teachers have become preoccupied with "coverage." . . . One of the most meaningful steps a school can take to promote significant improvement is to develop a process for identifying significant curriculum content, eliminating non-essential material, and providing teachers with time to teach the significant curriculum.[1]

By saying no to unimportant or less important things, educators are afforded more time and resources to be dedicated to the most important things.

#4: Leader in Me enables teachers to spend less time dealing with behavior-related problems. One benefit we commonly hear is that by spending ten minutes or so a day working on the habits and the culture of the classroom and school, teachers save far more than that amount of time not having to deal with disciplinary matters. Less time disciplining means more time for academics, teaching leadership skills, and enjoying school.

#5: Leader in Me improves teacher effectiveness and efficiency. As administrators and teachers apply the habits to their personal and professional lives, they become more effective and efficient. For example, as they share leadership responsibilities with students, they save time. Recall the teacher who used to spend twenty to thirty minutes closing down her classroom at the end of each day and now does it in two minutes with the help of her students. Sharing responsibilities frees up time for higher priorities, such as relationship building, planning, and doing other things leaders do.

These are five reasons why *Leader in Me*, if implemented with fidelity, can be a better way of doing what educators are already doing, and not just "one more thing."

See, Do, Get—The *Leader in Me* Framework

The best way we know to summarize *Leader in Me* and what we have covered in this book is to review the *Leader in Me* framework. Following the See, Do, Get model, it starts with how people SEE things, the five core paradigms. It then looks at how the paradigms influence the best practices that educators DO to address the three common challenges: leadership, culture, and academics. Applying those best practices with fidelity leads schools to GET positive, measurable results in all three areas: leadership, culture, and academics. (See the *Leader in Me* framework below.) It represents a whole-school, whole-student approach to school transformation that is implemented and sustained over time. If educators want to GET different results than they are currently achieving, they need to start to SEE and DO things differently. They cannot keep seeing and doing the same old things and expect to be getting different results.

Leader in Me Framework

	Paradigm of Leadership	Paradigm of Potential	Paradigm of Change	Paradigm of Motivation	Paradigm of Education
SEE Core Paradigms	Everyone can be a leader.	Everyone has genius.	Change starts with me.	Empower students to lead their own learning.	Educators and families partner to develop the whole person.

	Leadership	Culture	Academics
DO Highly Effective Practices	**Start with Adults Learning & Modeling** • Principal & Coordinator Development • New & Ongoing Staff Learning • Family & Community Partnerships **Teach Students to Lead** • Direct Lessons • Integrated Approaches • Service Learning	**Create a Leadership Environment** • Physical Environment • Social-Emotional Environment • Leadership Events **Share Leadership** • Lighthouse & Action Teams • Leadership Roles • Student Voice	**Achieve Goals** • Individual Goals • Team Goals • Aligned School Goals **Empower Learners** • Leadership Portfolios • Student-Led Conferences • Empowering Instruction
GET Measurable Results	Highly effective students and adults who are leaders in their school and community.	A high-trust school culture where every person's voice is heard and their potential is affirmed.	Engaged students who are equipped to achieve and entrusted to lead their own learning.

If you have not begun already, the next step is to get started. Start applying the concepts in this book in your classroom, school, district, family, and community. For assistance, reach out to one of our professionally trained coaches for support. Draw from their deep experience with the various challenges and levels within the field of education. Working with eight thousand schools across the globe, they have learned much about implementing *Leader in Me* in most any situation. They will help you adapt the principles and best practices to your specific needs.

Live Life in Crescendo

In the opening tribute to Dr. Covey, we shared his motto: "Live life in crescendo." He always lived and worked as if his greatest contribution was yet ahead. Millions of adults the world over now acknowledge him for having helped them better their lives. Students are now also becoming the beneficiaries of his work. At the end of his life, when Dr. Covey was asked what his greatest professional legacy would be, he thought for a moment and then quietly said, "The work we are doing with children with *Leader in Me*."

At the conclusion of his speeches, Dr. Covey often paused and quoted from memory the words of George Bernard Shaw:

This is the true joy in life. That being used for a purpose recognized by yourself as a mighty one. That being a force of nature instead of a feverish, selfish little clod of ailments and grievances complaining that the world will not devote itself to making you happy. . . . I want to be thoroughly used up when I die. For the harder I work the more I live. . . . Life is no brief candle to me. It's a splendid torch which I've got to hold up for the moment and I want to make it burn as brightly as possible before handing it on to future generations.[2]

We hope this book has been an opportunity for you to pause and reflect on how to best teach and prepare young people for life. And, just as important, we hope you have seen how this book applies to you and your choices as an educator. How might you bring the ideas and concepts contained in these pages to your school, your community, and your home? How might you inspire others to find their voice? What contributions will be a part of your crescendo?

Too many leaders are resigned to staying with the status quo. They are confined to what worked in the past. School change starts with individual change.

It is not for casual spectators. It is an inside-out process that starts with one's self. It can be very rewarding to teachers who have joined the profession to make a difference in students' lives.

In today's global economy, we simply cannot afford to continue waiting until young people receive their first job or promotion to a leadership position (including as a parent) before we teach them how to get along with others, to set goals, to think ahead. We cannot idly wait for them to become schoolteachers, doctors, firefighters, software engineers, and so forth before we teach them how to organize their lives, to take initiative, or to work in teams. We cannot afford to relax and expect that they will detect their worth and potential on their own. They deserve better. They deserve to be offered a source of hope.

You may be their one source of hope on your journey down the *Leader in Me* path. Please join us in preparing our students for a world that no one can possibly predict.

An Adult Lighthouse Team gathers to share insights and plans for enhancing *Leader in Me* initiatives at their school.

We hope you enjoyed the book . . .

If you have not begun already, the next step is to get started. Start applying the concepts in this book in your classroom, school, district, family, and community. For assistance, reach out to one of our professionally trained coaches for support. Draw from their deep experience with the various challenges and levels within the field of education. Working with eight thousand schools across the globe, they have learned much about implementing *Leader in Me* in most any situation. They will help you adapt the principles and best practices to your specific needs.

Acknowledgments

No project of this scope is without the contributions of many individuals. We recognize the literally hundreds of educators at *Leader in Me* schools around the world who have offered content expertise, quotations, photos, stories, and creative artistry. This book is truly the outcome of synergy.

Significant contributions were made by the dynamic headquarters, regional, and international teams, led by Sarah Noble Flokstra, Aaron Ashby, Joshua Covey, Gina Tanner, Zac Cheney, Anna Thompson, Brooke Griffin, Shelly Rider, Lonnie Moore, David Ansbacher, Josh Jefferson, Debra Lund, Janita Andersen, Christine Eisenhauer, Meg Thompson, Brooke Judd, William McIntyre, Gina Tanner, and Don Zegler. Much gratitude is expressed to the relentless support of FranklinCovey's CEO, Paul Walker, and our outstanding board of directors.

Careful input was provided by our professional team of consultants and coaches, including Dr. Nancy Moore, Gary McGuey, Jan McCartan, Charles Fonbuena, William Blackford, Dr. Lesley Eason, Maria Fleming, Robin Sampson, Dana Penick, Mike Suto, Chad Smith, Kim Yaris, Dr. Eve Miller, Tia McIntosh, and Dr. Jill Scheulen, as well as our magnificent client partners in the US and business partners around the globe. Special recognition is extended to the late John Flokstra, who contributed so much joy and so many creative resources to the *Leader in Me* family and worldwide community. We wouldn't be who we are without him.

We further recognize the numerous stories and quotes shared by our amazing team of Legacy Schools' principals, including Juley Sexton, Dr. Kim Cummins, Shirley Conde, Melody Hazeltine, Jennifer Million, Brett Shelby,

Jason Bennett, Cris Edwards, Keli Sare, Katie Booth, Jenadene Gray, Michael Wakefield, Matt Thornhill, Rebecca Jones, Sandra Oliveira, Ben Frasier, Tricia Murphy, Pauletha Butts, Cheryl Day, Beth Waufle, Brian Bradshaw, Jennifer Hanna, Rhonda Henry, Cathy Choate, Marjie Pippin, Brandy Bishop, Melissa Pender, and Glenda Mouskhajian.

We could not achieve what we have achieved without the meticulous guidance of our internal publishing team of Adam Merrill, Michèle Jessica "MJ" Fievre Logan, Meg Hackett, and Annie Oswald, nor the contributions of our friends at Dupree Miller & Associates, particularly Shannon Marven, and the outstanding editing leadership of Ian Straus and the entire professional team at Simon & Schuster.

Foremost, we extend our heartfelt appreciation to our families, whose consistent support throughout the project has sustained our energies. And, most importantly, we express gratitude for the millions of students for whom this work is dedicated. They give us hope, teach us about joy, and provide the inspiration to pursue this work.

Notes and References

In Tribute

1. Covey, S. R. (1989). *The 7 Habits of Highly Effective People: Powerful Lessons in Personal Change.* Simon & Schuster.

2. Cover, S. R., Covey, S., Summers, M. T., & Hatch, D. K. (2014). *The Leader in Me: How Schools and Parents Around the World Are Inspiring Greatness, One Child at a Time.* Free Press.

1: Rippling Across the World

1. The list of qualities and skills that employers seek that was given to Muriel was credited to the National Association of Colleges and Employers.

2. Covey, S. (1998). *The 7 Habits of Highly Effective Teens: The Ultimate Teenage Success Guide.* Simon & Schuster.

2: Seeing, Doing, and Getting in New Ways

1. Barth, R. S. (2013, October). "The Time Is Ripe (Again)." *Educational Leadership,* 71(2), 10–16.

2. The Emerson quote originally appeared in his collection of essays *Letters and Social Aims* but was later popularized and paraphrased in Dale Carnegie's classic *How to Win Friends and Influence People.*

3. Covey, S., Kosinski, L., & Thompson, M. (2023). *The 4 Disciplines of Execution for Educators: Achieving Your Wildly Important Goals.* FranklinCovey.

4. Sainz, A. J. (2021). The Leader in Me and Its Effects on School Culture and Leadership (Publication No. 28966047) [Doctoral Dissertation, Lindenwood University]. ProQuest Dissertations Publishing.

5. Crews, G. (2022). An Appreciative Inquiry of the Leader in Me: Understanding Implementation Experiences and Program Impacts via the Perspectives of Students, Teachers, and Administrators (Publication No. 28964065) [Doctoral Dissertation, University of North Carolina at Greensboro]. ProQuest Dissertations Publishing.

6. White, M. (2018). A Quasi-Experimental Study of the Effect of the Leader in Me on Attendance and Discipline in Missouri Schools. Survey Research Center, Institute for Social Research, The University of Michigan. https://www.leader inme.org/wp-content/uploads/2023/02/Attendance-A-Quasi-Experimental-Stu dy-of-the-Effect-of-the-Leader-in-Me-on-Attendance-and-Discipline-in-Missouri -Schools.pdf

7. Dethlefs, T., Green, M., Molapo, T., Opsal, C., & Yang, C. D. (2017). *Evaluation of the Leader in Me in the Cedar Valley.* Leader Valley Foundation. https://www .leaderinme.org/wp-content/uploads/2023/01/WEB-Evaluation-of-the-Leader in-Me-in-the-Cedar-Valley-Report.pdf

8. Bolden, P. (2019). An Evaluation of the "Leader in Me" Program Implementation in a Central Georgia Elementary School [Doctoral Dissertation, Valdosta State University]. Vtext Repository. https://vtext.valdosta.edu/xmlui/bitstream/han dle/10428/4217/boldenpatricia_dissertation_2019.pdf?sequence=1&isAllowed=y

9. Laird-Arnold, K. N. (2022). A Case Study of Cultural Awareness Integration Throughout the Elementary Education Curriculum [Doctoral Dissertations and Projects, Liberty University]. Digital Commons. https://digitalcommons.liberty .edu/cgi/viewcontent.cgi?article=4904&context=doctoral

10. Dick, S. J., Burstein, K., & Bergeron, M. (2017). The Leader in Me Evaluation: Phase 1 [Executive Summary]. United Way of Acadiana, University of Louisi- ana Lafayette. https://www.leaderinme.org/wp-content/uploads/2023/02/2017 _Leader-in-Me-Evaluation-Report_-Phase-1.-2016-2017-EVALUATIONREPO RT-Dick._Dick.pdf

11. Dethlefs et al. (2017).

12. Shetty, S., & D'Souza, F. C. R. (2021). "Impact of Stephen Covey's Seven Habits on the Academic Achievement of Secondary School Students." *International Journal of Multidisciplinary Educational Research* 10(1), 105–108.

13. Villares, E., Miller, A. E., & Chevalier, J. (2023). "The Impact of *Leader in Me* on the School Climate and Student Behaviours." *International Journal of Education Policy & Leadership* 19(2). https://doi.org/10.22230/ijepl.2023v19n2a1339

14. Bergin, C., Tsai, C.-L., Prewett, S., Jones, E., Bergin, D. A., & Murphy, B. (2024). "Effectiveness of a Social-Emotional Learning Program for Both Teachers and Students." *AERA Open,* 10. https://doi.org/10.1177/23328584241281284

3: Teaching Leadership Principles

1. Covey, S. R. (2005). *The 8th Habit: From Effectiveness to Greatness*. Free Press.

2. Covey, S. (2008). *The 7 Habits of Happy Kids*. Simon & Schuster.

3. Viorst, J. (1987). *Alexander and the Terrible, Horrible, No Good, Very Bad Day*. Atheneum Books for Young Readers.

4. Park, L. S. (2011). *A Long Walk to Water*. HarperCollins.

4: Creating a Leadership Culture

1. Robinson, Ken. (2009). *The Element: How Finding Your Passion Changes Everything*. Viking.

2. Hatch, D. K., & Summers, M. T. (2025). *Teacher Believed in Me: The Science and Heart of Making a Difference in Students' Positive Well-Being*. Simon & Schuster.

5: Aligning for Academic Results

1. Covey, S., Kosinski, L., & Thompson, M. (2023). *The 4 Disciplines of Execution for Educators: Achieving Your Wildly Important Goals*. FranklinCovey.

2. Ben-Shahar, T. (2007). *Happier: Learn the Secrets to Daily Joy and Lasting Fulfillment*. McGraw-Hill, p. viii.

6: Bringing It Home

1. Covey, S. R. (2022). *The 7 Habits of Highly Effective Families: Building a Beautiful Family Culture in a Turbulent World*. St. Martin's Essentials.

2. Covey, S. M. R. (2022). *Trust and Inspire: How Truly Great Leaders Inspire Greatness*. Simon & Schuster.

3. Hatch, D. K., & Summers, M. T. (2025). *Teacher Believed in Me: The Science and Heart of Making a Difference in Students' Positive Well-Being*. Simon & Schuster.

7: Engaging the Community

1. Fullan, M. (1997). "Broadening the Concept of Teacher Leadership." In S. Caldwell (Ed.), *Professional Development in Learning-Centered Schools*. National Staff Development Council.

8: Keeping It Alive

1. FranklinCovey's *The 4 Essential Roles of Leadership* is a workshop that has been applied with organizations around the world for over two decades. A book by the same name is currently in progress.

2. Deming, W. E. (1982). *Out of the Crisis*. Massachusetts Institute of Technology Press.

3. Thoreau, H. D. (1854). *Walden*. Thomas Y. Crowell.

9: Ending with the Beginning in Mind

1. Marzano, R. J. (2003). *What Works in Schools: Translating Research into Action*. Association for Supervision and Curriculum Development (ASCD). As a basis for his comments, Dr. Marzano references a TIMSS study by Schmidt, W., McKnight, C., & Raizen, S. in 1996.

2. Quotation is from *Man and Superman: A Comedy and Philosophy*, a play written in 1903 by George Bernard Shaw, and has been republished in many compilations over the years.

About the Authors

Dr. Stephen R. Covey

Stephen Covey is an internationally acclaimed leadership authority, consultant, and teacher. He is author of several renowned books, including the international bestseller *The 7 Habits of Highly Effective People*, which was named the #1 Most Influential Business Book of the Twentieth Century, selling more than forty million copies in thirty-eight languages. Other bestsellers include *The 8th Habit: From Effectiveness to Greatness*, *First Things First*, *Principle-Centered Leadership*, *The 7 Habits of Highly Effective Families*, *The Third Alternative*, and *Everyday Greatness*.

Dr. Covey received the National Speakers Association Speaker of the Year recognition, the Fatherhood Award from the National Fatherhood Initiative, the Thomas More College Medallion for continuing service to humanity, the Toastmasters Golden Gavel Award, the Sikh's International Man of Peace Award, and the International Entrepreneur of the Year Award. Dr. Covey was also recognized as one of *Time* magazine's 25 Most Influential Americans and received eight honorary doctorate degrees. He is cofounder and former vice chairman of FranklinCovey Company. He passed away during preparations for the second edition of *The Leader in Me* and is dearly missed, though his legacy carries on.

Dr. Covey is honored posthumously here due to his passing in 2012.

Sean Covey

Sean Covey is a global education leader, business executive, bestselling author, and keynote speaker with a passion for helping people and organizations unlock their potential. As president of FranklinCovey Education, he leads the worldwide implementation of *Leader in Me*, a whole-school transformation model that is now in more than 8,000 schools across 70+ countries.

A #1 *Wall Street Journal* and *New York Times* bestselling author, Sean has sold over ten million copies of his books, including *The 4 Disciplines of Execution*, *The 7 Habits of Highly Effective Teens*, *The 7 Habits of Happy Kids*, *The Leader in Me*, and *The 6 Most Important Decisions You'll Ever Make*. His work has been translated into more than thirty languages and is used by students, schools, and organizations across the globe.

Sean is a dynamic speaker known for connecting with audiences of all kinds—from students to CEOs—bringing a message that is both practical and inspiring. He regularly speaks on leadership, school transformation, culture, and goal-achievement, and his work has been featured in major media outlets worldwide.

Sean Covey is a Harvard MBA and former BYU quarterback who led his team to two bowl games. He is the cofounder of *Bridle Up Hope*, a nonprofit dedicated to inspiring hope, confidence, and resilience in young women through equestrian training. Sean and his wife, Rebecca, cherish time with their growing family of children and grandchildren.

Muriel Summers

Muriel Summers holds a BA degree from UNC–Chapel Hill, a master's in elementary education from UNC–Charlotte, a master's in school administration from the University of Maryland, and an honorary doctorate from California University. As a principal, Ms. Summers created the first leadership-based elementary school in the US. Her school, A.B. Combs Elementary, has received many national awards under her guidance, including: the National Blue Ribbon, the National School of Character, the National Magnet School of America, the National Title 1 Distinguished School, and the National Elementary School of the Year, as well as being designated as the inaugural lighthouse school by FranklinCovey Education. Ms. Summers was awarded the William and Ida Friday award for Leadership in Innovation, The Order of the Long Leaf Pine given by the Governor of North Carolina (the state's highest honor given to a North Carolinian), the University of North Carolina at Chapel Hill Award for Leadership in Education, and the Ralph Kimmel Award (North Carolina's highest honor for principals). She now serves as the global ambassador for *The Leader in Me* and keynotes at conferences across the United States and abroad.

Dr. David K. Hatch

Dr. David K. Hatch is a global thought leader for Franklin Covey Education. His doctorate in social-organizational psychology has led him to a fascinating career in corporate, government, and public education, and taken him to more than forty countries. He is coauthor of *Everyday Greatness* with Dr. Covey and was the lead researcher for the first, second, and now this third edition of *The Leader in Me*. Dr. Hatch's latest book, *Teacher Believed in Me*, is inspiring teachers' passions for making a difference in students' lives and increasing their readiness to learn. He resides in Utah with his wife, Mary Ann. They are dedicated to making the world a little happier for young people everywhere.

About FranklinCovey Education

For over three decades, FranklinCovey Education, a division of FranklinCovey and a global leader in education solutions, has been one of the world's most prominent and trusted providers of educational-leadership solutions. FranklinCovey's programs, books, and content have been utilized by thousands of public and private primary, secondary, and post-secondary schools and institutions, including educational service centers and vocational schools in all 50 states within the United States and in over 60 countries.

Our Mission

To enable greatness in students, educators, and school communities everywhere.

Our Vision

Our vision is to profoundly impact education across the globe by reaching every teacher and child in every corner of the world with our life-changing content. We believe it is our stewardship and responsibility to advance Leader in Me to become the most influential school system in the world.

Our PK–12 Solutions

- **Leader in Me:** A comprehensive PK–12 model designed to build leadership in students, create a high-trust culture, and improve academic achievement.
- **Professional Development:** Such as The 7 Habits of Highly Effective People®, The 4 Essential Roles of Leadership®, and Teacher Believed in Me.
- **Coaching:** Optimize productivity, personal effectiveness, and leadership skills in your school and district leaders.
- **Strategy Execution:** Use The 4 Disciplines of Execution® process to achieve success in your strategic priorities.

LeaderinMe®

Developing Life-Ready Leaders®

Every student possesses inherent greatness and unique potential. They deserve opportunities to develop leadership and life skills that prepare them for success in the future, but many schools are not set up to unleash that potential.

100+
independent research studies demonstrate our impact

8,000+
Leader in Me Schools

60+
countries served

20 million+
students reached

Leader in Me is FranklinCovey Education's comprehensive, evidence-based PK–12 model. It provides schools and districts with:

- A leadership and life-readiness framework for all students.
- The tools to create a high-trust school culture.
- A system for increasing academic achievement.

www.leaderinme.org

Books that Shape Leaders at Every Age

Bestselling books from FranklinCovey that have helped millions grow — at home, at school, and at work.

- *The Leader in Me*
- *Teacher Believed in Me*
- *The 7 Habits of Highly Effective Teens*
- *The 7 Habits of Happy Kids*
- *The 7 Habits of Happy Kids* Boxed Set
- *The 7 Habits of Highly Effective People: 30th Anniversary Edition*
- *The 6 Most Important Decisions You'll Ever Make*
- *The 4 Disciplines of Execution for Educators*

Available wherever books are sold.

Teacher Believed in Me

Through this professional development, teachers ignite or re-ignite their passions for making a difference in students' lives through actionable, evidence-based practices that:

- Build connections with students.
- Teach meaningful life lessons that resonate beyond the classroom.
- Inspire students to discover and develop their unique strengths.
- Entrust students with responsibilities that build self-worth.
- Support students with empathy and optimism when they face challenges.
- Empower students to take ownership of their learning and growth.
- Provide correction and feedback in positive, constructive ways.

Teacher Believed in Me is complementary to Leader in Me, FranklinCovey's flagship whole-school leadership model. For more information, visit LeaderinMe.org.

based on the new book

Book a Speaking Engagement

Looking to ignite real change in your school, district, or organization? Sean Covey and Muriel Summers—creators of the global Leader in Me model—deliver transformational keynotes that inspire action, build trust, and leave lasting impact.

Sean Covey

Bestselling author and President of FranklinCovey Education, Sean is known for his groundbreaking work on *The 7 Habits of Highly Effective Teens* and *The Leader in Me*. His powerful messages of personal leadership, potential, and cultural transformation have reached millions worldwide.

Muriel Summers

Former principal of A.B. Combs Leadership Magnet Elementary, Muriel was the visionary behind the very first Leader in Me School. Her passion for empowering students and educators impacts thousands of schools around the globe that are now implementing this model.